Curried Pasta with Mussels (page 120)

About the Authors

Coleen and Bob Simmons live in the San Francisco Bay area and have an active interest in food and wine. They have taken cooking classes from a variety of experts, have written a number of books and articles on wine, and teach cooking classes. Coleen is a space planner for a large research organization and Bob is an engineer.

A modern collection of quick, nutritious pasta recipes

- Featuring lighter ideas for pasta salads, soups, appetizers and main courses.

- Emphasis on fresh, easy-to-find ingredients.

- Tips on making your own flavored pasta, plus a special selection of extra-quick sauces.

- Recommendations for appropriate wines.

- For easy use, this book lies flat when opened, contains one recipe per page and is printed in large easy-to-read type.

- Compact design—takes a minimum of counter space.

Dedication

"To Bobbie Greenlaw with many thanks for her inspiration and assistance."

Quick & Easy PASTA Recipes

by Coleen and Bob Simmons

©Copyright 1983
Nitty Gritty Productions
P.O. Box 5457
Concord, California 94524-0457

A Nitty Gritty Cookbook
Printed by Mariposa Press
Concord, California

Library of Congress Catalog Card
Number, 83-061790
ISBN 0-911954-79-1

2nd Printing

Editor: Jackie Walsh
Art Director: Mike Nelson
Illustrator: Joan Baakkonen
Photographer: Glen Millward
Food Stylist: Bobbie Greenlaw

Special thanks to **The Williams-Sonoma
Mail Order Department** (San Francisco, CA)
and to **Creative Cookware etc.** (Concord, CA) for
the cookware and props in our photographs.

Table of Contents

Introduction 9
Pasta Basics
   The Right Ingredients 10
   Making Your Own Pasta 16
   Cooking Pasta 25
   Pasta Variations 27
Extra Quick Pasta Sauces 37
Easy Everyday Dishes
   Savory Appetizers And Soups 57
   Innovative Pasta Salads 71
   Pasta With Fresh Vegetables 87
   Pasta With Seafood 109
   Pasta With Chicken And Meat . . . 131

Traditional Favorites 155
   Manicotti 156
   Lasagne 158
   Cannelloni 160
   Ravioli 164
   And More 171
Glossary 181
Equivalents 184
Index 188

Introduction

Enjoy pasta often with a clear conscience—it's good for you! Pasta is being rediscovered as a satisfying, wholesome food, not high in calories, that can be served quickly and in many different ways with a wide variety of other healthful foods.

Pasta was once thought of as being fattening and too starchy to be good for you, but no longer. Times have changed! With ever-increasing health consciousness and the desire of many people to reduce their dietary intake of saturated fats, salt and preservatives, pasta is a perfect choice. A satisfying portion of pasta (about two ounces of dried pasta or three ounces of fresh pasta before cooking) has slightly more than 200 calories before the addition of a sauce or seasoning. The seasonings can be very pungent because the taste moderates when mixed with the blandness of pasta. Therefore, assertive foods such as garlic, strong cheeses and hot peppers can be used in small amounts to give today's pasta a delicious flavor without adding large numbers of calories.

Include pasta and pasta dishes in your menus often. In the pages to follow, you'll find enough recipes and ideas to last a long time. We hope you will enjoy them.

◀ **Shrimp and Dill Sauce** (page 113)

Pasta Basics

The Right Ingredients

ABOUT FLOURS:

Unless the recipe asks for a specific type of flour, all the pasta recipes in this book can be made with all-purpose flour. If it is available, unbleached bread flour makes a firmer pasta with more of a ''bite'' like the Italian pastas. Semolina or hard wheat durum flours can be substituted for at least part of the flour in most recipes. The best semolina flour is finely ground and should be specifically labled as being for pasta. Pasta made with semolina flour will require extra liquid, and needs to rest longer before being rolled out. The dough is difficult to roll out by hand, but works very well in a roller-type machine.

ABOUT EGGS:

Always use the freshest eggs available. The eggs used in the recipes in this book are Grade A large. Eggs vary slightly in size and composition from dozen to dozen, and even from egg to egg. **If using other than large eggs, mix the yolks and whites gently and use three tablespoons of the mixture for each**

egg called for in the recipe. Eggs at room temperature blend the best with flour.

ABOUT OILS:

Many recipes call for the addition of olive oil to the pasta dough. This tends to tenderize the dough and make it easier to roll out. This can be a *neutral* olive oil or any other mild salad oil such as corn or peanut. When olive oil is used in a sauce, a *fruitier* olive oil will add special character and flavor. Many fine imported olive oils are now available, usually labled "cold pressed extra virgin."

ABOUT TOMATOES:

The perfect fresh tomato for use in pasta sauces is the Romano or Italian. It is slightly oval, about the size of a large egg, and has very few seeds. Unfortunately this tomato is available fresh for only two or three months of the year. The next best tomato is the perfectly ripe salad tomato which has been peeled and seeded. If good quality fresh tomatoes are not available, buy a good brand of canned Italian plum tomatoes, preferably packed in rich tomato juice. There are good domestic brands available as well as imported.

Unless you have a great surplus of tomatoes there is no reason to start with fresh tomatoes for sauces that require long simmering. The end result is a little different from that made with canned tomato sauce or tomato paste.

If you are using canned tomatoes, hold the tomato over a sieve which has been set in a small bowl. With a small knife cut out the hard stem end and discard. Cut tomatoes in half lengthwise, and gently squeeze to remove most of the seeds. Place tomatoes on chopping board. After all of the tomatoes have been seeded pour the juice remaining in the can through the sieve. If the recipe does not call for the tomato juice, reserve it for another purpose. Chop the tomatoes and add to the sauce you are making at the last minute to preserve their best color and texture.

ABOUT PEPPERS:

The distinctive taste of peppers, whether they are red, green or yellow, mild or hot, fresh or dried, cooked or raw, complements the bland taste and smooth texture of pasta very well. The Italians often add a few red pepper flakes to a simmering sauce, or sprinkle a few flakes over a completed dish. Your taste will have to determine the amount used. People who love spicy food can eat and enjoy dishes

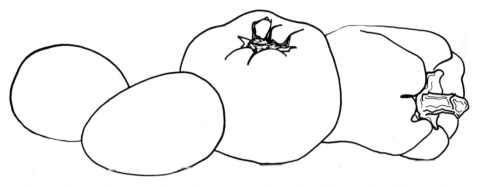

that would make others turn red and go running for the water faucet.

Many recipes call for red or green bell peppers. These can be used without peeling, but most recipes will be greatly improved if the peppers are peeled. The very best way to peel a pepper is to cut the pepper into quarters along the natural depressions and peel it with a sharp vegetable peeler. Then remove the seeds and ribs and cut the pepper into desired pieces. Peeled peppers cook more rapidly, stay crisper and tend to be easier on sensitive digestive systems.

ABOUT CHEESES:

The very best hard cheese to grate over pasta is aged Italian Parmigiano-Reggiano. It is dry but not grainy and the flavor is assertive, but not sharp. Not only does it taste better, but it is also more economical to buy Parmigiano by the piece at a good Italian delicatessen or cheese specialty shop and grate it fresh as needed. A chunk of ungrated cheese will keep for months in the refrigerator. Beware of "imported Parmesan," "imported Italian," and "Italian-type" cheeses, especially if sold grated, because these will invariably be inferior to the real Parmigiano.

The other Italian cheese often used with pasta is Romano which is made from sheep's milk. It has a much more assertive flavor than Parmigiano and tends to be more salty. It is better used in sauces and stuffings than as a grating cheese.

Good cheese stores often have other cheeses well enough aged to be properly dry and mellow for grating over pasta. Aged provolone, Gouda, Monterey jack, asiago, and sapsago all work well when grated fresh over pasta. The grated cheese sold in shaker top cans in supermarkets may be adequate for use in sauces, but should only be used as a last resort for other purposes.

Vegetable Lasagna (page 104) ▶

MAKING YOUR OWN PASTA

The best pasta you will ever eat is that which you make fresh at home! Salt, oil and egg content can be controlled according to the tastes and dietary needs of the people who will eat it. Here is an excellent and easy basic recipe with detailed instructions on mixing, rolling and cutting pasta using a variety of machines and techniques.

BASIC HOMEMADE EGG PASTA

This recipe makes slightly over a pound of delicious pasta.

2 cups all-purpose flour
1/2 tsp. salt
3 large eggs at room temperature (see page 10)

2 tbs. olive oil
1 or 2 tbs. water if needed

MIXING PASTA DOUGH

Mixing pasta by hand: Combine flour and salt. Place in a dome on the counter or mixing surface. Make a well in the flour. Break eggs into the well. Add olive oil, and with a kitchen fork gently beat the eggs and stir a little of the flour from the edges into eggs. Continue stirring until the eggs and flour are fairly well combined and mixture is too stiff to continue stirring with a fork. Gently knead in the rest of the flour with your hands, adding as much water as necessary to incorporate all the flour. Knead the dough in the same manner as you would for bread dough, pushing, folding and turning for about 10 minutes or until dough is smooth and elastic. You will find handmade pasta dough is more difficult to knead than bread dough. Don't despair, it will relax as it rests for easier rolling. Cover the dough and let it rest at room temperature for at least 15 to 20 minutes, but up to two hours is not too long.

Mixing pasta with a heavy duty mixer: Use any of the pasta recipes in this book. Place all ingredients in mixing bowl. Beat with paddle or kneading hook until dough forms a ball and cleans the sides of the mixing bowl. Turn out of bowl and if dough is still sticky, knead in a little flour. Wrap dough in plastic wrap and allow to rest for 20 minutes before rolling and cutting.

Mixing pasta in a food processor: The food processor makes easy work of mixing a one-pound recipe of pasta dough. With the metal blade in place, combine the flour and salt in the food processor bowl and pulse a few times to mix well. Break eggs into measuring cup. Add the olive oil and other liquid ingredients. Pour through the feed tube while the processor is running. If everything is perfect, in about 15 to 20 seconds all the ingredients will be mixed and the sides of the bowl will be clean. The pasta will have the texture of coarse meal, but will hold together when pinched between the thumb and forefinger. It should not stick to the fingers. **If the pasta is dry or not completely mixed** add a teaspoonful of water, process for a few seconds more, and check again. **If the pasta dough is sticky,** add more flour a tablespoon at a time until the proper consistency is reached. Remove the dough from bowl, and gather into a ball. Because the food processor has already partially kneaded the dough you will only have to knead it a minute until smooth. Wrap dough in plastic wrap. **Allow it to rest for 20 minutes or longer before rolling out.**

ROLLING PASTA DOUGH

Rolling by hand: Divide the rested dough into two or three pieces. Dust a heavy rolling pin with flour and roll one piece of dough at a time on a lightly floured surface. Keep the remaining dough covered with a damp paper towel to

prevent it from drying out. Roll dough into a large thin circle by continuing to roll from the center to the edges. When the dough is approximately 1/8-inch thick, make a final rolling to make the dough paper-thin. To do this, stretch the dough sideways with your hands while you roll back and forth with the rolling pin in this manner: Start with the far edge of the dough and lay about a fourth of the circle over the rolling pin. As you are rolling it towards you, quickly slide your hands out to the ends of the rolling pin back and forth very rapidly. Turn the rolling pin 90 degrees, cover it with another quarter of the dough and repeat the process. Continue until the whole circle of dough has been stretched. Repeat the rolling and stretching until dough is paper-thin and almost transparent. Do not roll dough for more than 10 minutes or it may become dry and lose its elasticity. Repeat rolling and stretching process with the remaining pieces of dough.

Letting hand-rolled dough rest: Hand-rolled dough should be allowed to rest for a few minutes before cutting. To do this place a clean towel on the counter, allowing about one-third of the towel to hang over the edge. Place the pasta circle on the towel, with approximately one-third of the pasta hanging over the side. Turn circle every 10 minutes. The dough will dry in approximately 30 minutes. The pasta is ready to cut when it is dry to the touch and looks slightly leathery. Drying the dough before cutting will help prevent the cut noodles from sticking together.

Rolling with a roller-type machine: There are **two kinds of roller machines: hand-cranked and electric.** Both knead and roll the pasta dough in the same way. The advantage of the electric machine is that you have two free hands for handling the dough. Just recently a motor attachment for the hand-cranked machine has become available.

After the pasta dough has been mixed either by hand, with a heavy duty mixer, or with a food processor as directed in Mixing of Pasta Dough, page 16, let it rest 15 to 20 minutes. Then divide the dough into two or three pieces and knead with the machine instead of by hand. This is done by setting the pasta machine rollers at the widest setting and running the dough through the machine until it becomes smooth and pliable. Fold the dough in thirds after each pass, and run through the machine again. When the dough is supple and very smooth, set the rollers to the next narrowest setting, fold the dough in half, and run through the rollers two times. Set the rollers to the next narrowest setting and repeat rolling and narrowing until the desired thickness is reached. If using the electric roller machine, use the narrowest setting only if you are making won ton squares or phylo dough, as this setting produces an extremely thin dough.

CUTTING PASTA DOUGH

Cutting by hand: Roll the dry, but still pliable, dough circle loosely into a flat roll about 3-inches wide. Cut pasta with a very sharp knife into desired widths. Press down evenly and cut, keeping the slices as even as possible. Don't saw. As soon as the whole roll has been cut, unroll so the noodles can dry further. **Fettuccine** is cut approximately 1/8-inch wide; **noodles** can range from 1/8-inch to 1-inch; **lasagne** is cut 1-inch wide or wider, or can be cut into squares; **manicotti** and **canneloni wrappers** are made by cutting pasta dough in **3- or 4-inch squares.** The squares are cooked and then wrapped around a filling to form a cylinder.

Cutting pasta with a hand-cranked roller machine: Allow the rolled out pasta dough (see page 20) to dry for 15 minutes before cutting. Remove the smooth rollers and fit the machine with the desired cutting attachment. Before running dough through cutting rollers, cut sheets of pasta into strips that fit the machine and the length you want the finished pasta to be. Lightly flour dough if it is at all sticky, and run through cutter roller.

It is important that you **NEVER** wash your roller machine. It should be carefully cleaned with a soft brush. The dried particles will fall out easily.

Cutting pasta with an electric roller machine: This machine operates exactly as the hand-cranked machine. Follow the same directions. The advantage is that you have two free hands for handling the strips of pasta. It also gets the job done in a hurry. **NEVER** wash this machine. Brush the dried particles out with a soft brush.

Your pasta is now ready to cook, or it can be stored in the refrigerator well-wrapped for several days before being cooked; or it can be dried thoroughly and stored in an airtight container for several weeks.

Lemon Pasta Soup (page 65) ▶

DRYING PASTA

If you've just made a batch of delicious pasta, you're probably going to want to eat it as soon as possible. However, it is possible to make it ahead of time and let it dry. Once pasta is thoroughly dry, it can be stored in an airtight container just as though it were a commercial product. To dry, take strands of pasta and loop them around your fingers. Let dry on a kitchen towel or cookie rack. Or, hang the long strands on a rack, or over the back of a chair, or even on a clothes drying rack. Also, there are a number of interesting commercial pasta drying racks now on the market. It usually takes pasta about 4 to 6 hours to dry.

EXTRUDER PASTA MACHINES

There are **two types of extruder pasta machines** available. **One type attaches to a heavy-duty mixer or food processor** and extrudes mixed pasta dough into desired shapes. The pasta dough can be mixed in the mixer or food processor and then forced through the extruder dies on the pasta attachment. For the pasta dough to extrude properly it may be necessary to have a softer dough than one that is perfect for a roller machine. Since each machine is different, a little testing may be needed before you get your dough just right. All recipes in this book should work well in extruder attachments.

The second type of extruder machine, such as the Simac, Moulinex Regal, or Osrow, mixes the pasta dough ingredients, and then at the flip of a switch or removal of a gate, extrudes the dough through one of many available dies. These machines work best with all-purpose flour or semolina flour. The consistency of the dough is very important to assure proper machine operation. Follow the manufacturer's directions exactly.

COOKING PASTA

Start with a large, deep kettle. **Use approximately six quarts of water and two tablespoons of salt for each pound of pasta.** Bring water to a full rolling boil and keep it boiling while pasta is cooking. It is not necessary to break long pasta as it will soften and slide into the water. Do not cover the pot while cooking pasta. **Do not overcook pasta.** It should be firm to the bite, but not too chewy. **Dried homemade pasta cooks in 5 to 6 minutes. Fresh homemade pasta is usually done in 2 to 3 minutes. Commercial dried pasta generally takes about 8 minutes to cook.** Follow the package directions for each variety. The only way to tell when pasta is cooked "to the bite" or "al dente" is to periodically fish out a strand and bite it. For homemade fresh pasta, start tasting soon after the water returns to a boil. For commercial dried pasta, start tasting a minute or two before the package directions say it will be done. Do not stir pasta with a spoon while it is cooking because this can cause it to stick together. Use a long-handled fork for a quick stir once or twice during the cooking. Drain pasta into a large strainer. **Do not rinse pasta that will be served hot. Do not allow it to become dry in the strainer,** and save a few tablespoons of the cooking water to add to the pasta if it seems dry after it has been sauced. Have a warm serving dish ready. Pour pasta into serving dish, add the sauce, toss to combine, and serve immediately.

Keeping cooked pasta hot until serving: Pasta is always best when cooked, drained and sauced immediately before serving. If an unexpected delay occurs, cooked, well-drained pasta can be kept warm for no more than 30 minutes by returning it to the hot cooking pot. Toss with two tablespoons of softened butter, cover the pot and place in a "warm" to 200-degree oven until ready to sauce and serve. Undercook the pasta by a minute or two if you anticipate that serving may be delayed. Unsauced leftover pasta is best reheated by immersing briefly in boiling water immediately prior to saucing.

Pasta Variations

Finest Egg Noodles

Makes one pound

Rich and golden, these noodles combine a silky smoothness with a delightful texture. They are perfect served with a little melted butter and freshly grated cheese.

2 cups all-purpose flour
1/2 tsp. salt
1/2 tsp. dry mustard
1 whole large egg
6 large egg yolks

Mix ingredients by hand, in a heavy-duty mixer, or food processor as directed on page 16. Wrap the dough in plastic wrap and allow to rest for at least 20 minutes before rolling and cutting (see pages 19 through 22).

Egg Pasta With Semolina Flour

Pasta made with semolina flour is perfect for lasagne and cannelloni. The texture is firmer than pasta made only from all-purpose flour. This pasta works best when mixed in a heavy-duty mixer or food processor, then rolled out in a roller machine (see pages 17 through 22).

2 cups semolina flour
1 tsp. salt
1 tbs. olive oil
2 large eggs
2 to 3 tbs. water

Mix ingredients in a heavy-duty mixer or food processor. Wrap the dough in plastic wrap and allow to rest for at least 20 minutes before rolling and cutting (see pages 19 through 22). The dough may seem to be dry and tend to crumble at first, but after a few passes through the machine it will come together.

28   Pasta Variations

Whole Wheat Pasta

Makes one pound

This recipe uses regular whole wheat flour. If stone-ground flour is substituted, it may be necessary to add more water.

2 cups whole wheat flour
1 tsp. dry mustard
1/2 tsp. salt
2 large eggs
approximately 1/4 cup water

Mix ingredients by hand, in a heavy-duty mixer, or food processor as directed on pages 16 through 18. Wrap the dough in plastic wrap and refrigerate for approximately 2 hours or overnight. Allow to come to room temperature before rolling and cutting (see pages 19 through 22).

Carrot Pasta

Carrots add a lovely golden color as well as flavor. This dough is soft enough to be easily rolled out by hand.

1/2 cup carrot puree (2 to 3 carrots)
2-1/2 cups all-purpose flour
3 large eggs
2 tbs. olive oil
1/2 tsp. salt
1 to 2 tbs. water as necessary

Peel and cook carrots until very soft. Puree in blender or food processor. Press puree through a sieve to remove any remaining pieces. Measure out 1/2-cup puree and return to saucepan. Cook for a minute or two over very low heat to dry out as much as possible. Combine puree with remaining ingredients and continue as directed in basic recipe on page 16. Wrap dough in plastic wrap and allow to rest for at least 20 minutes before rolling and cutting (see pages 19 through 22).

Fettuccine Alfredo (page 42)▶

Spinach Pasta

This beautiful green pasta is delicious with only cheese and butter. Also, try it with any of the vegetable or seafood sauces.

1/2 cup spinach puree (1/2 package frozen spinach)
2-1/2 cups all-purpose flour
3 large eggs
2 tbs. olive oil
1/2 tsp. salt
pinch nutmeg
1 to 2 tbs. water as necessary

Cook spinach and drain very thoroughly. Puree in blender or food processor. Press through a sieve to remove any bits of stem. Measure out 1/2 cup puree and return to saucepan. Cook for a minute or two over very low heat to dry out as much as possible. Combine with flour, eggs, olive oil, salt and nutmeg. Continue as directed in basic recipe on page 16. Wrap dough in plastic wrap and allow to rest for at least 20 minutes before rolling and cutting (see pages 19 through 22).

Red Pepper Pasta

This is a lovely pale pink pasta with a slight tang. Serve with scallops or shrimp for a pretty color and flavor contrast. It also addes a special zest to Fettuccine Alfredeo, page 42.

2 tbs. boiling water
2 tsp. dried hot pepper flakes (or more to taste)
2 cups flour
1/2 tsp. salt
1 tbs. oil
1 tbs. tomato paste
2 eggs

Put pepper flakes in small bowl and pour boiling water over. Let steep for 15 minutes. Combine flour and salt in food processor bowl and pulse a few times to mix. With processor running, add pepper flakes and water, tomato paste and eggs. Continue as directed in basic recipe on page 16. Wrap dough in plastic wrap and allow to rest for at least 20 minutes before rolling and cutting (see pages 19 through 22).

Green Chile Pasta

Here is a mildly spicy pasta variation which is delicious as a side dish with roasted meats. Be sure to drain the green chiles very well on paper towels before adding to the pasta mixture.

2 cups all-purpose flour
1 can (4 ozs.) whole green chiles, drained and seeded
1/2 tsp. salt
1/4 tsp. Tabasco sauce
1 large egg plus 2 egg yolks
1 tbs. olive oil

Combine flour, well-drained chiles, salt and Tabasco in food processor bowl. Process until smooth. (If you are using a mixer, puree the chiles in the blender before combining with the flour.) With the processor running, add olive oil and eggs. Process until dough has texture of coarse meal. Pinch dough between thumb and forefinger. The dough should stay together but not be sticky. Continue as directed in basic recipe on page 16. Wrap dough in plastic wrap and allow to rest at least 20 minutes before rolling and cutting (see pages 19 through 22).

Lemon Pasta

Makes one pound

Here is a light lemony pasta that goes beautifully with seafood or as an accompaniment to spiced dishes in place of rice. It is also delicious in salads.

2 cups all-purpose flour
1/2 tsp. salt
2 large eggs
2 tbs. vegetable oil
finely grated rind of 1 lemon
1/4 cup lemon juice

Mix ingredients by hand, in a heavy-duty mixer or food processor as directed on page 16. Wrap the dough in plastic wrap and allow to rest for at least 20 minutes before rolling and cutting (see pages 19 through 22).

Extra Quick Pasta Sauces

Bell Pepper and Anchovy Sauce 45
Bobbie's Walnut Sauce 51
Butter and Cheese Sauce 39
Classic Garlic and Oil Sauce 38
Creamy Nut Sauce 52
Fettuccine Alfredo 42
Four-Cheese Sauce 44
Fresh Tomato and Garlic Sauce 47
Creamy Gorgonzola Sauce 43
Parsley Sauce 50
Pesto Sauce 48
Spaghetti Carbonara 54
Spicy Pepperoni and Mushroom Sauce 53
White Wine and Butter Sauce 42
Zesty Tomato and Hot Pepper Sauce 46

Extra Quick Sauces

In this section, we have included extra quick sauces that can be made from start to finish in less time than it takes to boil the water and cook the pasta. They use a variety of ingredients such as shrimp, clams, vegetables, nuts and cheese.

When making these quick sauces, assemble the ingredients first, because there won't be time once you start cooking. Put the appropriate amount of water (at least six quarts for one pound of pasta) in a large pot and start it heating; then start the sauce. The amount of pasta for a serving, and how much sauce to put on it, is an individual preference. In general, 12 ounces of fresh pasta, or 8 ounces of dried pasta will make 3 to 4 medium servings when cooked.

All pastas are complemented by a sauce. It may be simple or a more complicated one, it doesn't matter. The blandness of pasta enables it to blend perfectly with a large variety of other foods. There are many suitable cheeses for grating over hot pasta (see The Right Ingredients, page 10). For a perfect treat anytime, try tossing grated Fontina, mozzarella, Gouda or a mild cheddar and two tablespoons melted butter with hot, well-drained pasta.

Think of pasta first when you're looking for something really quick, easy and satisfying, and always serve it on warm plates.

Pasta with
Classic Garlic and Oil Sauce

This is the simplest of all pasta preparations for any kind of pasta. Serve with roasted, broiled or barbequed meats.

12 ozs. fresh **or** 8 ozs. dried pasta
1/4 cup fruity olive oil
2 to 3 cloves garlic, finely chopped
1/2 tsp. dried basil
1/4 cup chopped parsley, Italian if available
salt and freshly ground black pepper

While the pasta is cooking, warm olive oil in a small saucepan. When it is quite warm, remove from heat and add remaining ingredients. The oil should not be so hot that the garlic browns. Let steep until the pasta is done. Pour hot well-drained pasta into a warmed bowl and toss with sauce. Serve immediately with another grinding of fresh black pepper.

Pasta with
Butter and Cheese Sauce

Preparation time: 15 minutes
Servings: 3 to 4

With only butter and cheese in the refrigerator, you can make this delicious, satisfying sauce. Try it with Finest Egg Noodles, page 27.

12 ozs. fresh **or** 8 ozs. dried pasta
1 stick (1/4 pound) unsalted butter
1/2 tsp. dried oregano **or** basil
salt and freshly ground pepper
1/2 cup freshly grated Parmesan cheese

While the pasta is cooking, heat butter gently in a small pan until barely melted. Add herbs, salt and pepper. Pour half the herb-butter into a warm bowl. Add cooked, well-drained pasta and quickly toss. Pour the remaining sauce and one half of the cheese over pasta. Toss until cheese is incorporated and starts to melt. Add remaining cheese and toss until mixed thoroughly. If the pasta appears to be dry add one or two tablespoons of the hot pasta cooking water and toss to blend. Serve immediately on warm plates. *Wine suggestion: Pinot Blanc or Napa Gamay*

Pasta with
White Wine and Butter Sauce

Use this superb sauce alone or with seafood, chicken or vegetables. It has a delightful silky texture and delicate flavor.

12 ozs. fresh **or** 8 ozs. dried spaghettini
   or tagliarini
1/3 cup shallots, minced
2/3 cup dry white wine **or** dry vermouth
2 tbs. lemon juice

8 tbs. (one stick) unsalted butter
white pepper
2 tbs. minced parsley
6 ozs. cooked chicken or shrimp,
   cut into match-sticks (optional)

Have pasta cooking water boiling and ready when needed. Place shallots and white wine in a small heavy saucepan. Reduce wine over high heat until only 2 to 3 tablespoons remain. Remove pan from heat and let stand for 3 or 4 minutes. Start pasta cooking. While pasta is cooking, place pan with shallots and wine over very low heat. Add lemon juice. Divide butter into 8 thin slices. Add one butter slice at a time and whisk vigorously until butter is absorbed. Repeat with remaining slices. Remove pan from heat occasionally while beating in the butter. If the pan gets too hot, the butter sauce will separate. Add shrimp or chicken to sauce. Serve over hot, well-drained pasta on warm plates. *Wine suggestion: Chardonnay or Dry Riesling*

Preparation time: 15 minutes
Servings: 3 to 4

Fettuccine Alfredo

This recipe for a simple cream and cheese sauce tossed with freshly cooked pasta is a classic.

12 ozs. fresh **or** 8 ozs. dried fettuccine
2 tbs. butter
3/4 cup heavy cream
1/2 cup Parmesan cheese
freshly grated nutmeg
salt and freshly ground pepper

While pasta is cooking, melt butter in a large skillet. Add cream and 1/4 cup cheese. Simmer over very low heat 4 to 5 minutes until sauce starts to thicken. Drain pasta well and add to skillet. Lift and stir to combine all ingredients and coat the pasta. Add remaining cheese, nutmeg, salt and a generous grinding of black pepper. Serve on warm plates.

Variation: Add 1/4 tsp. hot pepper flakes to skillet when butter has melted.

Pasta with
Creamy Gorgonzola Sauce

This is a great side dish for roast or grilled meats, or serve it as a first or main course with a full bodied red wine.

12 ozs. fresh **or** 8 ozs. dried pasta
2 tbs. butter
3 ozs. Gorgonzola **or** other blue-veined cheese
1/2 cup cream
white pepper
parsley for garnish

While pasta is cooking, place butter, Gorgonzola cheese, cream and pepper in a small saucepan. Gently cook over low heat, stirring constantly, until cheese melts and forms a smooth sauce. Pour hot, well-drained pasta into a warm bowl. Toss with sauce and top with parsley. Serve immediately on warm plates.

Wine suggestion: Cabernet Sauvignon or Zinfandel

Pasta with
Four-Cheese Sauce

Four favorite cheeses are combined with cream and seasonings for an easy and delicious sauce. Cheeses may be varied according to whim and availability.

1 lb. fresh pasta **or** 12 ozs. dried pasta
1 tsp. butter
1 garlic clove, crushed
1/2 cup heavy cream
1/4 cup freshly grated Parmesan cheese
1/2 cup grated Gruyere **or** Swiss cheese

1/4 cup cream cheese
1/4 cup blue-veined cheese
1/2 tsp. white pepper
salt
nutmeg
parsley for garnish

While pasta is cooking, melt butter in small saucepan. Saute garlic clove until it starts to turn color. Remove garlic and discard. Add cream, Parmesan, Gruyere, cream cheese and blue cheese to saucepan. Cook over very low heat, stirring constantly until cheeses melt. Add pepper, salt and a dash of nutmeg. Toss immediately with hot well-drained pasta. Serve on warm plates. Sprinkle with chopped parsley.   *Wine suggestion: Slightly chilled Grenache Rose or Zinfandel Blanc*

Pasta with
Bell Pepper and Anchovy Sauce

This subtle sauce will appeal even to those who are not terribly fond of anchovies.

12 ozs. fresh **or** 8 ozs. dried vermicelli **or** tagliarini
1/4 cup olive oil
1 can (2 ozs.) imported anchovy fillets with oil
2 ozs. unsalted butter
2 cloves garlic, finely chopped
2 medium bell peppers, one red and one green, peeled and cut into strips
chopped parsley and freshly grated Parmesan cheese

While pasta is cooking, place olive oil, anchovies including their oil, butter and garlic in small saucepan. Heat gently. Do not allow garlic to brown. Mash anchovies until they dissolve. Add pepper strips and gently simmer for two minutes. Drain pasta and pour into a warm bowl. Pour sauce over pasta and mix well. Serve on warm plates. Sprinkle with chopped parsley and freshly grated cheese.

Variation: Add 1/4 teaspoon hot pepper flakes to olive oil mixture.

Pasta with
Zesty Tomato and Hot Pepper Sauce

For the very best flavor use fresh Romano tomatoes if they are available, or small regular tomatoes.

8 ozs. dried **or** 12 ozs. fresh fettuccine **or** tagliarini
6 to 8 Romano tomatoes, peeled
1/3 cup fruity olive oil
2 tsp. minced garlic
1 tsp. oregano
1 to 2 small fresh hot peppers, finely chopped
salt and pepper
freshly grated Parmesan cheese

While pasta is cooking cut tomatoes in quarters and remove seeds. Heat olive oil in a large skillet. When hot add tomatoes, garlic, oregano, hot peppers, salt and pepper. Saute over medium heat 4 or 5 minutes, or until tomatoes are soft but still hold their shape. Toss with hot well-drained pasta in warm bowl. Serve immediately. Pass Parmesan cheese.

Pasta with
Fresh Tomato and Garlic Sauce

This uncooked sauce must be made at least one hour before serving and allowed to stand at room temperature to develop the flavors.

8 ozs. dried **or** 12 ozs. fresh spaghetti **or** tagliarini
3 large ripe tomatoes, peeled, seeded and coarsely chopped
2 tbs. chopped fresh sweet basil
1 tbs. chopped fresh chives
2 tbs. chopped Italian flat-leaf parsley **or** cilantro
3 garlic cloves, finely chopped
1/3 cup fruity olive oil
1/2 cup finely grated Mozzarella **or** Fontina cheese
salt and freshly ground pepper
freshly grated Parmesan cheese

Time the pasta so it will be done just before it's to be mixed with the sauce. Combine tomatoes, basil, chives, parsley, garlic, olive oil, cheese, salt and pepper in a medium-size bowl. Let stand approximately one hour before serving. Cook pasta. Combine sauce and hot, pasta in warm bowl. Pass Parmesan cheese.

Pasta with
Pesto Sauce

Fragrant fresh sweet basil leaves, garlic, walnuts or pine nuts and olive oil make a delicious sauce for homemade pasta.

1 lb. fresh pasta **or** 12 ozs. dried pasta	3/4 cup fruity olive oil
2 cups fresh basil leaves	3/4 cup freshly grated Parmesan cheese
3 large cloves garlic	1/2 tsp. salt, or to taste
3/4 cup chopped walnuts **or** pine nuts	freshly ground pepper

While pasta is cooking, place fresh basil leaves, garlic, nuts and olive oil in food processor bowl or blender container. Process until ingredients are well mixed, scraping down sides of container once or twice. Process until mixture is fairly smooth. Pour into bowl and stir in cheese, salt, and pepper. Toss with hot, well-drained pasta in warm bowl.

Variation: Cook 1 cup Rizo or other rice-shaped pasta according to package directions. Stir in 1/3 cup Pesto Sauce. Fill 4 hollowed-out, medium-size tomatoes with mixture. Top with Parmesan cheese and bake in 375°F. oven 15 minutes. Serve hot with barbequed lamb or steaks.

Pesto Sauce (page 48) ▶
Parsley Sauce (page 50)

Pasta with
Parsley Sauce

Preparation time: 15 minutes
Servings: 3 to 4

This sauce is particularly good with whole wheat pasta or fresh Oriental noodles. Use the food processor to chop the parsley and garlic.

12 ozs. fresh pasta **or** 8 ozs. dried pasta
3/4 cup butter
2 cloves garlic, minced
1 cup finely chopped parsley
salt and freshly ground pepper to taste
Parmesan cheese

Cook pasta while making sauce. Melt butter in a medium-size skillet. Add garlic and cook 1 minute. Stir in parsley, salt and pepper. Turn off heat and let stand until pasta is cooked and drained. Combine sauce with pasta in warm bowl. Pass Parmesan cheese.

Variation: Sprinkle with coarsely chopped, toasted walnuts, peanuts or almonds.

Pasta with
Bobbie's Walnut Sauce

This delicious, uncooked, nut sauce can be ready by the time the pasta is cooked with the help of a food processor or blender.

12 ozs. fresh pasta **or** 8 ozs. dried pasta
1 slice white bread, crusts removed
2 tbs. milk
1 cup walnuts
1/3 cup chopped parsley
2 garlic cloves, chopped

3 tbs. butter, softened
1/2 tsp. salt
1/4 tsp. hot red pepper flakes
1/2 cup olive oil
1/4 cup heavy cream (optional)

While pasta is cooking, soak bread in milk a minute or two. Squeeze bread dry and discard milk. Place walnuts, parsley and garlic in food processor bowl or blender container. Process until coarsely chopped. Add bread, butter, salt and red pepper flakes. With processor running, gradually add olive oil. If a thinner sauce is desired, add cream. Toss with hot, well-drained pasta. Serve on warm plates.

Pasta with
Creamy Nut Sauce

Serve over small shells or bowties, or with the Cheese Ravioli, page 169.

12 ozs. fresh pasta **or** 8 ozs. dried pasta
2 tbs. butter
1 large clove garlic, minced
2 tbs. flour
1-1/3 cups Swanson's beef **or** chicken broth
1/2 tsp. anchovy paste

1/4 tsp. white pepper
1/4 tsp. salt
1 cup walnuts, very finely chopped
1/3 cup heavy cream
parsley for garnish

While pasta is cooking, melt butter in small saucepan. Saute garlic for one minute. Add flour and cook 2 minutes. Gradually add broth, anchovy paste, pepper and salt. Cook until sauce thickens. Stir in walnuts and cream just before serving. Cook just long enough to heat sauce. Toss with hot, well-drained pasta in warm bowl. Sprinkle with chopped parsley.

Wine suggestion: Dry Riesling.

Pasta with
Spicy Pepperoni and Mushroom Sauce

This hearty sauce is perfect when you're hungry, but short on time.

12 ozs. fresh pasta **or** 8 ozs. dried pasta
1 tbs. oil
1/4 lb. pepperoni, skin removed and thinly sliced
1/2 lb. fresh mushrooms, thinly sliced
1/2 tsp. salt, or to taste
4 to 5 green onions
1/2 cup heavy cream

While pasta is cooking, heat oil in large skillet. Saute pepperoni 3 to 4 minutes. Remove and set aside. Add sliced mushrooms, salt and onions to skillet. Saute 4 to 5 minutes over medium heat until mushrooms are limp and onions are soft. Add cream and pepperoni and heat through. Combine with hot, well-drained pasta and serve immediately on warm plates.

Wine suggestion: Barbera or full-bodied Zinfandel

Spaghetti Carbonara

Here is a classic sauce with bacon, eggs and cream. If it is available, the Italian rolled bacon called Pancetta will add special character and flavor to this dish.

1 lb. fresh pasta **or** 12 ozs. dried pasta
1/2 lb. bacon **or** pancetta
1 large onion, chopped
1/2 cup finely chopped parsley
2 eggs, room temperature

3/4 cup freshly grated Parmesan cheese
1/4 tsp. hot pepper flakes (optional)
1/2 cup heavy cream
2 tbs. soft butter for pasta

Start heating pasta cooking water so it will be ready when needed. Cut bacon into 1-inch pieces. Saute in skillet until crisp. Remove bacon pieces. Pour off all but 2 tablespoons bacon fat. Saute onion in bacon fat 3 to 4 minutes until soft. Combine parsley, eggs, Parmesan cheese, pepper flakes and cream in small mixing bowl. Cook pasta and drain well. Toss with butter in a large warm bowl. Quickly pour egg mixture over hot pasta and mix. Add bacon and onion. Toss to combine. Serve immediately on warm plates.

Wine suggestion: A light, fruity Zinfandel or Napa Gamay

Savory Appetizers and Soups

Appetizer Won Ton 58
Clam and Spinach Appetizers. 59
Green Chile and Cheese Appetizers 60
Lemon Pasta Soup 65
Mexican Pasta Soup 68
Mushroom Pasta Soup 66
Oriental Noodle Soup. 61
Pasta and Cheese Soup 69
Pasta In Broth 64
Won Ton Soup 62

Savory Appetizers and Soups

While pasta was probably known in Italy long before Marco Polo returned from China, the Chinese have had several hundred years' experience with both boiled and fried pasta. The most familiar Oriental pastas are Chinese noodles and won ton wrappers, which are thin squares of Chinese noodle dough measuring about 3 inches. They are sold fresh in one-pound packages in the produce section of many supermarkets and can frequently be found in the frozen food department. There are 60 to 80 won ton wrappers per pound, depending on the thickness of the dough. Fresh wrappers will keep for a week or more in the refrigerator or they can be frozen and defrosted when needed.

Fried won ton appetizers can be made ahead, lightly browned in oil, cooled and then frozen in airtight containers. When you are ready to serve them, place on a rack in a shallow pan and bake in a 350°F. oven 10 to 15 minutes until hot and crisp. We have included our three favorites: Clam and Spinach, Green Chile and Cheese and a more traditional one with pork, shrimp and water chestnuts.

Pasta soups range from hearty to light and we have included a few of each. The Cold Lemon Pasta Soup, Pasta In Broth, Pasta and Cheese Soup and Mexican Pasta Soup all make delicious starters for a dinner. Seafood Stew and Mushroom Pasta Soup can be used as the entree for a soup and salad meal.

Appetizer Won Ton

Won ton can be fried for appetizers or simmered in broth for a hearty soup.

1/2 lb. ground pork
2 tsp. cornstarch
1 tbs. soy sauce
2 tsp. dry sherry
1 tsp. sesame oil
1 tbs. vegetable oil

3 to 4 small fresh shrimp, finely chopped
1 egg white
4 green onions, finely chopped
6 water chestnuts, finely chopped
50 to 60 won ton wrappers
oil for frying

Combine pork, cornstarch, soy sauce, sherry and sesame oil. Heat vegetable oil in skillet. Fry pork mixture 4 to 5 minutes, crumbling meat as it cooks. Remove meat from skillet with a slotted spoon or drain in a sieve to remove fat. Place meat in bowl. Add salt, pepper and shrimp. Stir in egg white, onions and chestnuts. Place 1 teaspoon filling in center of a won ton wrapper. (Keep unused wrappers covered with damp towel.) Moisten one- half of wrapper edge with water. Fold over to form a triangle, pressing firmly around edges to seal. Moisten left tip of triangle. Bring right tip around. Press tips together. Heat oil to 375°F. Fry won ton a few at a time until lightly browned. Drain on paper towels. Serve immediately.

Preparation time: 45 minutes
Makes about 3 dozen

Clam and Spinach Appetizers

Be sure to drain the spinach and clams very thoroughly, otherwise the filling mixture will be too moist.

4 green onions, thinly sliced
1 clove garlic, minced
1 tbs. butter
2 ozs. cream cheese **or** ricotta cheese
1/2 cup cooked, well-drained spinach
2 tbs. Parmesan cheese
1/2 tsp. salt

3 to 4 drops Tabasco
1 can (6-1/2 ozs.) minced clams, well drained
30 to 40 won ton wrappers
Parmesan cheese for topping
oil for frying

Saute onions and garlic in butter until soft. Combine cream cheese, very well drained spinach, sauteed onions, Parmesan cheese, salt and Tabasco in food processor bowl. Process until smooth. Stir in drained clams. Fill won ton wrappers according to directions for Appetizer Won Ton on page 58. Fry in deep fat until lightly browned. Drain well. Serve immediately sprinkled with freshly grated Parmesan cheese, if desired, or dip in seafood cocktail sauce. These can be fried, cooled and then frozen. Reheat on a rack in 350°F. oven for 15 minutes.

Green Chile and Cheese Appetizers

Won ton wrappers are used for this quick appetizer. Make ahead and keep in freezer until ready to reheat and serve.

2 tbs. canned green chiles,
  seeded and finely chopped
1 cup grated Parmesan cheese
4 ozs. cream cheese

1 egg yolk
50 to 60 won ton wrappers
oil for frying
taco sauce for dipping

Combine chiles, Parmesan, cream cheese and egg yolk. Chill in refrigerator 20 to 30 minutes for easier handling. Fill wrappers one at a time. (Keep unused wrappers covered with a damp towel.) Place 1 teaspoon filling in the center of a won ton wrapper. Moisten one-half of wrapper edge with water. Fold over to form a triangle, pressing wrapper firmly around edges. Wet left tip of triangle with a little water. Bring right tip around. Press together firmly. Heat oil to 375°F. Fry won ton a few at a time until very lightly browned. Drain on paper towels. Serve immediately with a mild taco sauce for dipping.

Oriental Noodle Soup

8 ozs. fresh Chinese-style noodles **or** 4 ozs. dried noodles
2 cans (14 ozs. ea.) chicken **or** beef broth
1/2 tsp. sesame oil
1 tbs. soy sauce
white pepper
1/2 cup diced cooked ham, chicken, pork **or** shrimp
1/2 cup frozen peas
5 green onions with 1-inch of green top, thinly sliced

Cook noodles in large pot of rapidly boiling water for 3 minutes. Drain well. Bring broth to boil in a large saucepan. Add drained noodles, sesame oil, soy sauce, white pepper, diced meat, peas and green onions. Cook 5 minutes. Serve immediately.

Variation: Add 1 cup coarsely chopped fresh spinach leaves in place of peas. Cook until leaves wilt.

Preparation time: 45 minutes
Cooking time: 15 minutes
Servings: 4

Won Ton Soup

Prepare the won ton as directed on page 58. Instead of frying them all, drop 20 to 25 won ton in this rich broth of a delicious, hearty soup.

4 cups chicken **or** beef broth
1 tbs. soy sauce
1/2 tsp. sesame oil
3 green onions finely chopped

1/2 tsp. pepper
20 to 25 filled won ton
1/2 cup frozen peas
1/2 cup cooked diced carrot

Bring broth to boil. Add soy sauce, sesame oil, onions and pepper. Reduce heat to simmer and add won ton. Gently simmer uncovered 12 to 14 minutes. During the last 6 minutes of cooking add peas and carrots. Serve in soup bowls, ladling 5 to 6 won ton into each bowl with broth.

Won Ton Appetizers (page 58) ▶
Won Ton Soup (page 62)

Pasta in Broth

If you don't have homemade broth available, here is a delicious substitute. Add pasta and you have a light soup.

2 cans (15 ozs. ea.) beef **or** chicken broth (or use one of each)
1/2 cup finely chopped onion
1/2 cup finely chopped carrots
1/4 cup finely chopped celery, including some leaves
1 bay leaf
2 or 3 black peppercorns
2 ozs. dried thin pasta (Riso, shells or other small shapes)

Combine broth, onion, carrots, celery and seasonings in a medium-size saucepan. Bring to boil and gently simmer uncovered for 20 minutes. Strain through a sieve or damp cheesecloth, pressing as much juice as possible out of the vegetables. Discard vegetables. Measure stock. If necessary add enough water to bring stock up to 4 cups. Return to saucepan. Bring to boil. Add thin pasta broken into 1-inch pieces, or riso, alphabets, or other small pasta. Cook until pasta is done. Serve immediately in warm bowls.

Lemon Pasta Soup

This soup can be served hot or cold, but it is particularly nice chilled and served in pretty glass bowls. Garnish with thin lemon slices.

1/2 cup tiny pasta shapes (stars or
  shells)
6 cups chicken broth
salt to taste

1/8 tsp. white pepper
3 eggs
1/3 cup lemon juice
1 lemon, thinly sliced for garnish

Combine pasta, chicken broth, salt and pepper in saucepan. Bring to boil. Cover and simmer until pasta is tender, about 10 minutes. Remove from heat. Beat eggs in separate bowl until pale yellow. Slowly add lemon juice to eggs. Carefully stir some of the hot broth into egg-lemon mixture, beating continuously. Add tempered egg-lemon mixture to remaining hot broth. If serving hot, ladle into hot soup cups and garnish with lemon. If serving cold, cool soup then refrigerate 3 to 4 hours or overnight. Serve very cold and stir well before ladling into serving bowls. Garnish each bowl with one or two thin lemon slices.

Mushroom Pasta Soup

This flavorful soup uses both fresh and dried Oriental mushrooms for a rich taste. Use a food processor to chop the vegetables and slice the mushrooms.

2 ozs. dried pasta (small shells, small macaroni or noodles)
2 dried Oriental mushrooms
3 cans (15 ozs. ea.) beef broth
1/2 cup finely chopped onion
1/2 cup finely chopped carrots
1/4 cup finely chopped celery, including some leaves
1 bay leaf
2 or 3 black peppercorns
2 tbs. butter
1/2 pound fresh mushrooms, thinly sliced
2 tbs. brandy
1/8 tsp. white pepper

Cook pasta according to package directions. Rinse with cold water, drain, and set aside. Cover dried mushrooms with boiling water and let stand for 5 minutes.

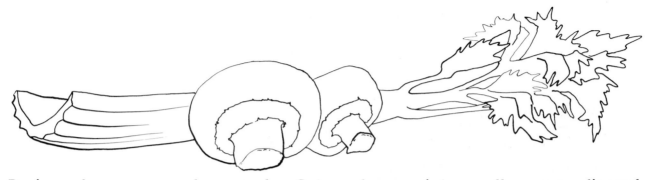

Drain and squeeze mushrooms dry. Cut mushrooms into small squares, discarding the hard stem. In a large saucepan combine beef broth, onion, carrots, celery, bay leaf and peppercorns. Bring to a boil and simmer uncovered for 20 minutes. Strain broth through a sieve or damp cheesecloth, pressing as much juice as possible out of the vegetables. Discard vegetables. Return broth to saucepan. Heat butter in a large skillet. When foaming add fresh mushrooms and the dried mushroom pieces. Saute over high heat 3 to 4 minutes until mushrooms are almost done. Pour brandy over mushrooms and continue to cook for another minute until mushrooms are fairly dry. Season with white pepper. Approximately 10 minutes before serving, add mushrooms to broth and bring to a boil. Add pasta and heat through. Serve in hot soup bowls garnished with parsley.

Mexican Pasta Soup

Creamy and mildly spicy, this makes a delicious winter soup.

3 ozs. dried pasta (small shells)
1 tbs. butter
6 green onions, thinly sliced
2 canned green chiles, or to taste
1 can (14 ozs.) chicken broth

1/2 tsp. dried cumin
1/2 tsp. salt, or to taste
1/4 tsp. white pepper
1 cup half and half
cilantro or chopped pimiento

Cook pasta according to package directions (if using thin pasta break in 1-inch pieces). Drain. Heat butter in small skillet. Saute onions until soft. Drain green chiles and remove seeds. Place chiles, sauteed onion and a little of the chicken broth in a food processor bowl or blender container and process until mixture is smooth. Bring chicken broth to boil in a medium saucepan. Add chile mixture, cumin, salt, pepper and cooked pasta. Add light cream and heat through. Pour into warm soup bowls and garnish with cilantro or pimiento. Serve immediately.

Preparation time: 15 minutes
Servings: 6 to 8 appetizers
or 4 entree

Pasta and Cheese Soup

This is an elegant cream soup that is a perfect starter for a holiday dinner, or a satisfying lunch or supper entree.

2 cans (14-1/2 ozs. ea.) chicken broth
1/2 cup dry white wine
3 ozs. very thin pasta (vermicelli or tagliolini)
2 tbs. soft butter
1/2 cup grated Monterey jack cheese

1/3 cup grated Parmesan cheese
3 egg yolks
3/4 cup heavy cream
parsley for garnish

Combine chicken broth and wine in saucepan. Bring to boil. Break pasta into 1/2-inch pieces and add to broth. Cook until pasta is almost done, about 8 minutes. While pasta is cooking, combine butter and cheeses. Add egg yolks and mix well. Add heavy cream to cheese-egg mixture. When pasta is almost cooked, remove saucepan from heat. Carefully stir a little of the hot broth into the cheese-egg mixture, beating continuously. Combine the tempered cheese-egg mixture with remaining broth. Serve immediately in warm cups or bowls. Garnish with parsley. *Wine suggestion: Medium dry sherry if serving as a first course*

Innovative Pasta Salads

Artichoke and Tortellini Salad 73
Blue Cheese Pasta Salad 74
Calamari and Dill Pasta Salad 84
Deli Pasta Salad 82
Hot Dogs and Wagonwheels 80
Macaroni Salad 76
Oriental Noodle Salad 78
Pasta Shells With Green Beans and Sardines 83
Pasta Salad With Green Beans and Walnuts 77
Patio Shell Salad 75

Pasta Salads

Pasta salads make splendid side dishes for steak, chicken, fish, ham or other meat entrees. They can also be the featured dish for luncheons, picnics and cold suppers.

Tender, delicate-flavored pasta complements the crisp, colorful vegetable pieces and slivers of meat that are often used in salads. The most piquant dressings are quickly absorbed and become wonderfully mellow as they chill.

This section features many easy and quick salads including our hearty Deli Salad made with cold cuts; flavorful Calamari and Dill Salad; subtle Oriental Noodle Salad; Hot Dogs and Wagonwheels Salad that particularly appeals to the younger set, and many other combinations.

Remember to prepare most pasta salads several hours ahead so they can chill and the flavors have time to harmonize. Stir the salads after an hour or so of chilling. If they appear dry, add a little more mayonnaise or oil to moisten. If salads are to be served outside it is important to keep them as cold as possible to avoid spoilage.

Preparation time: 30 minutes
Servings: 6 appetizer or
4 luncheon

Artichoke and Tortellini Salad

Use imported dried tortellini for this excellent appetizer or luncheon salad.

1 package (7 ozs.) dried cheese tortellini
3 or 4 artichoke bottoms **or** hearts
2 to 3 tbs. diced pimiento
2 tbs. chopped fresh sweet basil **or**
    1/2 tsp. dried
4 tbs. mayonnaise

2 tsp. Dijon mustard
1/4 cup grated Parmesan cheese
salt to taste
white pepper
2 tbs. chopped parsley

Cook tortellini as directed on package. Drain and rinse with cold water and drain well. Cook artichokes if fresh or frozen. If using marinated artichoke hearts, drain well. Cut artichokes bottoms into 1/4-inch slivers, and artichoke hearts into small pieces. Combine cooked tortellini, artichokes, pimiento and sweet basil with mayonnaise and mustard. Season to taste. Garnish with fresh parsley. Refrigerate until ready to serve. Add a little more mayonnaise if salad seems dry.

Variation: Add 1/4-cup small, cooked shrimp **or** thin squares of prosciutto.

◀ **Pasta Salad with Green Beans and Walnuts** (page 77)

Blue Cheese Pasta Salad

This salad is nice as a cheese course. Use Danish Blue, Roquefort, Stilton, or any blue-veined cheese. Make salad one to two hours ahead so flavors have time to develop.

12 ozs. fresh pasta **or** 8 ozs. dried pasta (corkscrews, wagon wheels
   or small shells)
4 ozs. blue-veined cheese, crumbled
2 cups walnuts, toasted and coarsely chopped
1 cup chopped celery
4 tbs. mayonnaise
1/8 tsp. white pepper
salt to taste
3 tbs. minced parsley

Cook pasta as directed. Immediately rinse with cold water and drain well. Add cheese, walnuts, celery, mayonnaise, pepper and salt. Gently toss with two forks until ingredients are well mixed. Refrigerate one to two hours. Add a little more mayonnaise if salad seems dry. Sprinkle with parsley. Serve slightly chilled.

Preparation time: 30 minutes
Servings: 6 to 8

Patio Shell Salad

This hearty salad features red kidney beans, yellow corn, green chiles and cumin for a South-of-the-Border flavor.

4 ozs. dried small pasta shells
1 can (15 ozs.) red kidney beans, well drained
1 can (12 ozs.) corn, well drained
4 to 5 green onions, finely chopped
4 to 5 tbs. canned green chiles, finely chopped
1/2 tsp. ground cumin

1 tsp. dried oregano
1 tbs. lemon juice
1/2 cup mayonnaise
1/2 tsp. salt
1/4 tsp. freshly ground
  black pepper

Cook pasta according to package directions. Drain and immediately rinse with cold water. Drain well and set aside. Rinse kidney beans under cold water and drain well. Rinse corn and drain. Combine pasta, kidney beans, corn, onions, chiles, cumin, oregano, lemon juice, mayonnaise, salt and pepper. Gently toss with two forks. Chill in refrigerator for at least two hours before serving. Add a little more mayonnaise if pasta seems dry.

Macaroni Salad

This is a perfect picnic salad. For even better flavor, make it several hours ahead and let it mellow in the refrigerator before serving.

1 cup uncooked salad macaroni
2 hard-cooked eggs, chopped
1 tbs. minced green onion
1/4 cup minced sweet pickle
1/4 cup finely diced celery
1 tbs. capers
1 cup cooked green peas
2 tbs. chopped pimiento

1/2 cup mayonnaise
2 tbs. pickle juice
1 tsp. prepared mustard
1/4 tsp. white pepper
1 tsp. salt
2 tbs. sour cream
2 tbs. minced parsley

Cook macaroni in boiling water for 12 minutes, or according to package directions. Drain and rinse with cold water. Drain well. Place in mixing bowl. Add chopped eggs, onion, pickle, celery, capers, peas and pimiento. Combine mayonnaise, pickle juice, mustard, pepper, salt and sour cream. Add to macaroni mixture. Add parsley. Toss lightly with two forks to combine. Chill before serving.

Pasta Salad With
Green Beans and Walnuts

Preparation time: 15 minutes
Servings: 4 to 6

8 ozs. corkscrew pasta
3 cups cooked fresh green beans
1 cup walnuts, coarsely chopped
4 tbs. olive oil
2 tbs. white wine vinegar
1 cup ham **or** salami, diced

4 green onions, thinly sliced
2 tbs. parsley, minced
1 tbs. dried dill weed **or**
   3 to 4 tbs. fresh dill, finely chopped
1/8 tsp. cayenne
salt to taste

Cook pasta, drain and immediately rinse with cold water. Drain well and pour into large bowl. Cut green beans in 1-inch pieces. Toss with pasta. Toast chopped walnuts in oven until hot to the touch. Combine olive oil and white wine vinegar. Pour over pasta and green beans. Gently toss with two forks. Add ham, walnuts, onions, parsley, dillweed, cayenne and salt. Toss well. Serve at room temperature or slightly chilled.

Oriental Noodle Salad

This is a flavorful salad using fresh Japanese noodles. Fresh Oriental noodles called "Udon" can be found in the produce section of most supermarkets. Substitute spaghetti or linguine if they are not available.

8 ozs. fresh Japanese noodles
2 tbs. vegetable oil
2 ozs. bacon, Pancetta **or** ham
2 tbs. red wine vinegar
1 tbs. sesame oil
1 tbs. soy sauce
2 cloves garlic, minced
1/2 tsp. red pepper flakes
2 green onions
1 large carrot

Cook noodles as directed on package, approximately 1 to 3 minutes. Drain and rinse with cold water. Drain and pat dry with paper towels. Toss with two tablespoons vegetable oil to keep noodles from sticking together. Saute bacon or

Pancetta until crisp and crumble into small pieces. If using ham, cut in 1/4-inch pieces. Combine red wine vinegar, sesame oil, soy sauce, garlic and red pepper in small sauce pan. Bring to boil and cook 2 minutes over medium heat. Cut white parts of green onions into long slivers. Coarsely grate carrot or cut into fine strips the same size as the onion. Combine noodles, bacon or Pancetta, vinegar sauce, green onions and carrot. Gently toss with two forks. Serve slightly chilled or at room temperature.

Variation: Substitute 1/2 cup small cooked shrimp and 1 cup finely diced celery for bacon or Pancetta, onion and carrot.

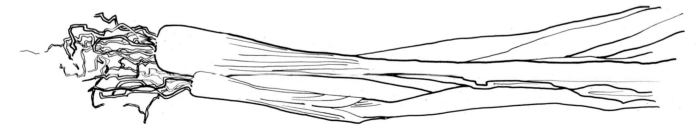

Hot Dogs and Wagonwheels

This is a whimsical salad that will be a sure hit with the kids. It makes great picnic fare.

6 ozs. wagonwheel pasta
5 all-beef hot dogs, boiled and sliced into thin rounds
1/3 cup thinly sliced sweet pickle
1/4 cup finely chopped green pepper
2 green onions, white part only, thinly sliced
1/2 cup mayonnaise
1 tbs. prepared mustard
2 tsp. vinegar
salt and pepper to taste
2 tbs. chopped parsley

Cook wagonwheels according to package directions. Drain and immediately rinse with cold water. Drain again well. Place hot dogs and pasta in large bowl. Add pickle, green pepper, green onions, mayonnaise, mustard, vinegar, salt, pepper and parsley. Gently toss with two forks. Chill in refrigerator at least two hours.

Preparation time: 30 minutes
Servings: 4 entree or
      6 to 8 first course

Deli Pasta Salad

8 ozs. dried egg noodles
3 ozs. Mortadella, ham **or** bologna, thinly sliced
3 ozs. Gruyere **or** Swiss cheese, thinly sliced
1 large sour **or** German-style pickle
1 large **or** 2 small tart apples, peeled
1-1/2 tbs. Worcestershire sauce
3 to 4 tbs. mayonnaise
1/2 tsp. white pepper
2 tbs. freshly grated Parmesan cheese
2 tbs. parsley, minced

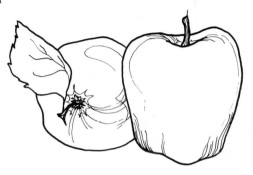

Cook noodles. Immediately drain and rinse with cold water. Drain well. Cut meats, cheese and pickle into strips approximately the same width and thickness as the noodles. Coarsely grate the apple. Combine noodles with meats, cheese, apple and pickle. Add Worcestershire sauce, mayonnaise, white pepper and grated cheese. Gently toss with two forks until well mixed. Refrigerate for at least two hours or overnight before serving. Garnish with minced parsley.

Pasta Shells With
Green Beans and Sardines

This is a colorful, savory picnic or luncheon salad. Marinate at least an hour before serving.

8 ozs. dried pasta shells **or** corkscrews
2 cans (4-3/8 ozs. ea.) sardines, drained
   and flaked
2 cups cooked green beans, cut in
   1-inch pieces
2 to 3 shallots, minced
2 to 3 tbs. capers, rinsed and drained

2 tsp. Dijon mustard
2 tbs. white wine vinegar
4 tbs. olive oil
1/2 tsp. freshly ground black pepper
10 to 12 cherry tomatoes
2 to 3 tbs. parsley, minced

Cook pasta. Drain and immediately rinse with cold water. Drain well and pour into large bowl. Add sardines, green beans, shallots and capers to pasta. Combine mustard, vinegar, olive oil and pepper. Pour over pasta and gently toss with two forks until well mixed. Spoon onto serving platter. Cut cherry tomatoes in half and remove seeds. Place in a ring around salad. Sprinkle top of salad with parsley.

Wine suggestion: Sauvignon Blanc

Calamari and Dill Pasta Salad

This salad makes an excellent first course or luncheon entree.

1/3 cup lemon juice
1/4 cup light olive oil
1-1/2 tsp. dried dill weed **or** 3 tbs. fresh dill, finely chopped
1/2 tsp. thyme
dash of cayenne pepper
1/2 tsp. salt, or to taste
8 ozs. dried small fusilli **or** shells
2 lbs. small fresh calamari
sour cream (optional)
cherry tomatoes and watercress

Make a marinade by combining lemon juice, olive oil, dill, thyme, cayenne and salt in a large bowl. Set aside. Cook the pasta as directed, drain and rinse with cold water. While pasta is cooking, clean the calamari by pulling off the head with the ink sac and removing the cellophane center inside the body. Rinse inside well under running water. Remove outside skin by rubbing under running water. Cut

into 1/4-inch rings. Bring a large pot of lightly salted water to a rapid boil. Add the calamari all at once. Cook over high heat for no more than 1 minute. Drain immediately. Pour hot drained calamari rings into a bowl containing the marinade. Toss to mix well. Add the cooked pasta to the calamari and toss again. Refrigerate for at least two hours before serving. Stir once or twice. When ready to serve toss with enough sour cream to lightly coat the salad, if desired. Serve on glass plates garnished with cherry tomatoes and watercress.

Pasta With Fresh Vegetables

Confetti Pasta 92
Pasta Oriental 101
Pasta Primavera 96
Pasta Provencal 94
Pasta With Carrots and Broccoli 88
Pasta With Fresh Zucchini 91
Pasta With Marinara Sauce 98
Pasta With Peas And Mushrooms 90
Pasta With Rich Mushroom Sauce 100
Spinach and Mushroom Pasta 102
Vegetable Lasagne 104
Zucchini and Pasta Casserole 106

Pasta With Fresh Vegetables

Vegetables with pasta make an attractive combination that offers a satisfying contrast of textures and is very pleasing to the eye. Red and green peppers, orange carrots, yellow and green squash, red tomatoes, green asparagus, snow peas and tiny peas instantly provide a colorful palette for the pale pasta. The vegetables in pasta dishes can be slightly cooked to provide a crunchy texture or cooked just long enough for the different flavors to harmonize so one ingredient is not prominent.

We like to peel and seed fresh tomatoes, and a relatively new technique to us—peeling red or green peppers with a vegetable peeler—was a delightful discovery because it preserves the crispness of the raw peppers and is quicker than the usual method of blistering the skin over flame and then peeling. But peeling vegetables is a personal preference. Your cooking pleasure should not be diminished by too many rules or special techniques.

In this section is a marvelous vegetable lasagne layered with mushrooms, carrots, peppers, eggplant and ricotta cheese; a striking confetti pasta with red and green pepper; and many other different vegetable combinations. Use the freshest vegetables in season and your own favorites to create delicious new variations.

Pasta with
Carrots and Broccoli

Preparation time: 30 minutes
Servings: 4 to 5

Crisp vegetables add interest to this quick and colorful pasta dish. Try it with zucchini instead of broccoli.

12 ozs. fresh **or** 8 ozs. dried pasta
4 medium carrots
3 cups broccoli pieces
5 green onions
4 to 5 strips bacon or Pancetta

2 tbs. olive oil
2 large cloves garlic, minced
1 tbs. red wine vinegar
2 tbs. melted butter

Start heating pasta cooking water in a large pot. Cut carrots into matchsticks approximately 1-1/2 inches long. Cut broccoli floweretes from stems and slice stems into paper-thin pieces. Thinly slice green onions. Saute bacon in a large skillet until crisp. Remove from pan and crumble into small pieces. Start pasta cooking. Pour out all but 2 tablespoons bacon drippings. Add olive oil to bacon drippings. When oil is hot add carrots, broccoli, green onions and garlic. Toss to coat vegetables with oil. Cover and cook for 1 to 2 minutes. Add vinegar and cook for another minute. Toss cooked, well-drained pasta with melted butter. Add vegetable mixture and toss to combine ingredients. Serve on warm plates.

Pasta with
Peas and Mushrooms

12 ozs. fresh **or** 8 ozs. dried linguine
5 ozs. blanched frozen peas
2 tbs. butter
1 clove garlic, minced
1 small onion, chopped
4 ozs. mushrooms, thinly sliced

4 ozs. ham, cut into long thin strips
1 teaspoon dried basil
3/4 cup half and half
salt and pepper
3/4 cup grated cheese

Bring pasta cooking water to boil in large pot. Cook pasta while making sauce. Drain well before using. Cook peas until almost done. Heat butter in skillet until foamy. Add garlic and onion and saute gently for two to three minutes. Increase heat and add mushrooms. Saute for two minutes. Add ham, basil, peas, cream, salt and pepper. Simmer gently for two to three minutes. Place hot, well-drained, pasta in a warmed bowl. Pour sauce over pasta. Add grated cheese one half at a time, mixing after each addition. If pasta seems dry, add a little more half and half. Serve on warmed plates. Pass more freshly grated cheese.

Variation: Add 1/4 cup chopped pimiento at the same time the peas are added.

Pasta with
Fresh Zucchini

Here is a flavorful crisp zucchini and tomato topping for pasta.

12 ozs. fresh pasta **or** 8 ozs. dried pasta
2 tbs. butter
1 medium onion, chopped
1 garlic clove, minced
3 medium zucchini
1 can (15 ozs.) tomato sauce

1/2 tsp. dried marjoram
1/2 tsp. dried oregano
1/2 tsp. dried sweet basil
1/2 tsp. salt
1/4 tsp. white pepper

Start heating pasta cooking water in large pot. Time pasta so it is cooked when the sauce is ready. Drain well before using. Melt butter in medium saucepan. Saute onion until soft but not brown. Add garlic. Slice zucchini in half lengthwise, then slice across in 1/4- to 1/2-inch slices. Add to onion and garlic. Stir in tomato sauce, marjoram, oregano, sweet basil, salt and pepper. Cover and simmer 15 minutes, stirring occasionally. Mix with hot, well-drained pasta.

Confetti Pasta

Fresh red and green peppers make this a colorful pasta dish. Peeling the fresh peppers with a vegetable peeler results in a crisp, crunchy texture very different from roasted peppers, and is worth the effort.

12 ozs. fresh pasta **or** 8 ozs. dried pasta
1 fresh red pepper
1 fresh green pepper
2 tbs. olive oil
1 small onion, chopped
2 cloves garlic, minced
1/2 cup tiny green peas, cooked
1/4 cup sliced ripe olives

1/2 tsp. dried oregano
1/2 tsp. dried sweet basil
3 tbs. chopped fresh parsley
1 cup cubed (1/4-inch) Fontina **or** other mild cheese
freshly ground black pepper
salt to taste
2 tbs. butter, melted

Start heating pasta cooking water in large pot. Cut peppers into vertical sections following the natural ridges. Remove the seeds and membrane. Using a vegetable peeler remove the thin outer skin. Cut into 1/4-inch squares or julienne. Start pasta cooking. Heat olive oil in medium-size skillet. Saute onion and garlic until soft but not brown. Add peppers. Cook one minute. Stir in green peas, olives, oregano, basil, parsley, cheese, salt and pepper and remove from heat. Toss cooked, well-drained pasta with melted butter. Add approximately one-half of the sauce, tossing with two forks. Top with remaining sauce and serve immediately on warm plates.

Variation: Add 1 cup diced ham or slivered salami.

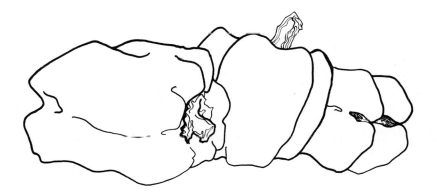

Pasta Provencal

Crisp eggplant and red pepper slivers make a quick, savory first course or luncheon dish.

12 ozs. fresh pasta **or** 8 ozs. dried spaghetti
2 Japanese eggplants **or** 1 small eggplant
flour
1/2 cup olive oil
1 red pepper, peeled and julienned

3 cloves garlic, minced
salt and pepper to taste
2 tbs. chopped parsley
Parmesan cheese

Start heating pasta cooking water in large pot. Time pasta so it is cooked when sauce is ready. Cut unpeeled eggplant into 1/4-inch slices, and then into 1/2-inch pieces. Lightly dust eggplant pieces with flour. Heat oil in a large skillet. When oil shimmers, add eggplant pieces and saute over medium heat for approximately 2 minutes until lightly browned on one side. Turn eggplant pieces over. Add red pepper slivers, garlic, salt and pepper. Saute for approximately 2 to 3 minutes until eggplant is crisp and lightly browned. Toss with hot, well-drained pasta. Top with parsley and serve immediately on warm plates. Pass freshly grated Parmesan cheese. *Wine suggestion: Gewurztraminer or dry Chenin Blanc*

Pasta Primavera

12 ozs. fresh **or** 8 ozs. dried tagliarini, spaghetti **or** fettuccine
2 medium-size tomatoes, peeled, seeded and coarsely chopped
4 tbs. olive oil
1 small onion, finely chopped
1/4 tsp. red pepper flakes
1/2 lb. mushrooms, thinly sliced
1 clove garlic, minced
1 cup diagonally sliced asparagus **or** green beans
1 cup caulifloweretes
1 medium-size yellow squash, thinly sliced
1 medium-size red **or** green pepper, peeled and cut in thin strips
1 cup coarsely grated carrots
1/2 cup fresh blanched **or** frozen peas
salt and pepper to taste
3 tbs. parsley, finely chopped
1/3 cup Parmesan cheese

Start heating pasta cooking water in large pot. Time pasta so it is cooked

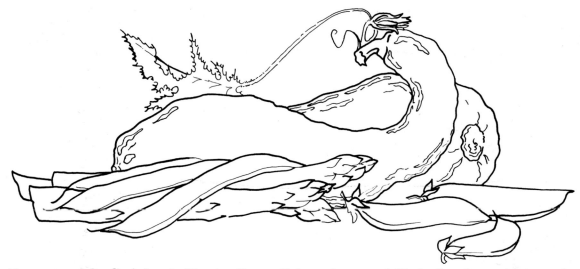

when the sauce is finished. Heat olive oil in a large skillet. Saute onion and red pepper flakes for 3 to 4 minutes. Add mushrooms and garlic. Cook for 2 minutes over medium-high heat. Add asparagus pieces, cauliflowerets, yellow squash and peppers. Cover and cook 2 minutes. Add carrots, tomato pieces, peas, salt and pepper. Cook 2 to 3 minutes. Toss with hot, well-drained pasta. Top with parsley and Parmesan cheese. Serve immediately on warm plates.

Preparation time: 15 minutes
Cooking time: 45 minutes
Servings: 4 to 5

Pasta with
Marinara Sauce

This easy, full-bodied sauce can be used alone over pasta, or combined with chicken, fish, pieces of pork or meatballs. It goes together in less than 15 minutes, but needs 45 minutes simmering time. Keep it on hand and you'll never be without a fast meal.

1 lb. fresh pasta **or** 12 ozs. dried pasta
1 large can (28 ozs.) Italian-style tomatoes
4 tbs. olive oil
1/2 cup onion, finely chopped
1/2 cup green pepper, finely chopped
1 large clove garlic
2 tbs. tomato paste
2 tbs. pimiento, diced
1/2 tsp. dried oregano
1/2 tsp. dried basil
dash cayenne

Have pasta cooking water hot and time the pasta so it will be done when the sauce is ready. Avoid letting the pasta wait after it is cooked. Drain well before using. Prepare tomatoes by draining them in a sieve placed over a large bowl. Cut out tough stem ends of tomatoes and squeeze out as many seeds as possible. Reserve tomato juice and chop tomatoes. Discard seeds in sieve. Heat oil in a large saucepan. Saute onions, green pepper and garlic over low heat for 8 to 10 minutes until onions and peppers are very soft but not brown. Add tomatoes and their juice, tomato paste, pimiento, oregano, basil and cayenne. Simmer over low heat, stirring occasionally, approximately 45 minutes or until the sauce is the desired consistency. Serve over hot, well-drained pasta on warm plates.

Wine suggestion: Barbera or Petite Sirah

Pasta with
Rich Mushroom Sauce

12 ozs. fresh pasta **or** 8 ozs. dried pasta
4 small dried black Oriental mushrooms
4 tbs. butter
3/4 lb. fresh mushrooms, thinly sliced
2 tbs. minced shallots
2 tbs. soy sauce

2 tbs. brandy
1 cup heavy cream
white pepper
salt to taste
2 tbs. chopped fresh parsley

Start heating pasta cooking water in a large pot. Place dried mushrooms in small bowl. Cover with boiling water and let stand 10 minutes. Squeeze dry. Cut into small thin slices. Melt butter in medium-sized skillet. When foaming add fresh sliced mushrooms and slivered dried mushrooms. Saute two to three minutes. Add shallots and cook for another minute. Add soy sauce, brandy, heavy cream and white pepper. Cook over medium heat approximately 4 to 5 minutes, or until sauce is reduced to almost one half its original volume. While sauce is reducing, cook pasta. Drain well. Toss sauce with cooked, drained pasta. Sprinkle with parsley, and serve immediately on warm plates.

Wine suggestion: Merlot or a rich Chardonnay

Preparation time: 30 minutes
Servings: 3 to 4

Pasta Oriental

Fresh snow peas and bean sprouts along with other garden vegetables make this a colorful and delicious main course.

12 ozs. fresh **or** 8 ozs. dried tagliarini
  or fettuccine
6 tbs. butter
1 small onion, finely chopped
1/2 tsp. red pepper flakes, or to taste
1/2 lb. fresh mushrooms, thinly sliced
2 cloves garlic, minced

1 cup thinly sliced yellow squash
1 cup thinly sliced zucchini
1 cup snow peas, strings removed
1 cup fresh bean sprouts
1 cup chopped tomatoes
3/4 cup heavy cream
salt and pepper to taste

Bring pasta cooking water to boil in a large pot. Cook pasta while making sauce. Melt butter in a large skillet. Saute chopped onion with red pepper flakes 3 to 4 minutes. Add mushrooms and garlic. Saute 2 minutes. Add yellow squash, zucchini, snow peas, bean sprouts, tomato pieces, cream, salt and pepper. Cook over high heat 2 to 3 minutes until cream starts to thicken and vegetables are crisp-tender. Drain pasta well. Combine approximately one half of the sauce with hot pasta. Top with remaining vegetables and sauce. Serve on warm plates.

Spinach and Mushroom Pasta

Puree cooked spinach and cottage cheese in a blender or food processor to make a lovely green pasta sauce.

12 ozs. fresh pasta **or** 8 ozs.
   dried spaghetti or linguine
2 tbs. butter
8 ozs. fresh mushrooms, thinly sliced
5 to 6 green onions, thinly sliced

1 cup cooked spinach, well drained
1 cup small curd cottage cheese
1/4 cup heavy cream
salt and white pepper to taste
Parmesan cheese for garnish

Start heating pasta cooking water in a large pot. Melt the butter in a medium-size skillet. When foaming, add mushrooms and saute 2 to 3 minutes. Add the green onions and cook for another minute. Place cooked, well-drained spinach, cottage cheese and heavy cream in a blender container or food processor bowl. Process until smooth. Combine with mushrooms and onions. Season with salt and pepper. Start pasta cooking. Just before pasta is done, heat the mushroom and spinach mixture. Combine with hot, well-drained pasta. Serve immediately on warm plates. Pass freshly grated Parmesan cheese.

Pasta Oriental (page 101) ▶

Vegetable Lasagne

This dish can be made a day in advance and reheated when needed.

Tomato Sauce, page 105
Vegetable Sauce, page 105

2 cups ricotta cheese
1/2 cup Parmesan cheese

Prepare Tomato Sauce and Vegetable Sauce. Cook lasagne noodles as directed. Drain and rinse with cold water. Drain well. Place one layer of cooked noodles in a buttered 9- by 13-inch baking dish. Top with one-half of vegetable sauce. Spread 1/2 cup ricotta cheese over vegetable layer. Top with another layer of noodles. Repeat vegetable and ricotta cheese layers. Pour about 1/3 cup tomato sauce over ricotta. Top with final layer of lasagne noodles. Spread with remaining ricotta cheese. Distribute remaining tomato sauce over cheese and top with Parmesan cheese. Bake in 350°F. oven 20 to 25 minutes until hot and bubbly. If lasagne is frozen, allow to defrost. Cover with foil and heat in 350°F. oven 30 minutes. Uncover and bake 10 minutes longer or until thoroughly heated and bubbly. Let stand about 10 minutes before cutting into serving pieces.

Wine suggestion: Zinfandel or Charbono

TOMATO SAUCE

1 can (15 ozs.) tomato puree
1 tsp. dried sweet basil

1 tsp. dried oregano
2 tbs. dry white **or** dry vermouth

Combine tomato puree, basil, oregano and white wine in small saucepan. Bring to a boil and simmer uncovered over medium heat 10 minutes.

VEGETABLE SAUCE

1/3 cup olive oil
1 cup finely chopped onions
1/4 to 1/2 tsp. hot red pepper flakes
1 lb. fresh mushrooms, coarsely chopped
2 cloves garlic, minced

2 cups coarsely grated carrots
1 green pepper, finely chopped
1 red pepper, finely chopped
1-1/2 cups peeled, diced eggplant

Heat olive oil in large skillet. Add onions and pepper flakes and saute 5 to 6 minutes until onions are soft but not browned. Increase heat. Add mushrooms and saute 3 to 4 minutes. Add garlic, carrots, peppers, eggplant, salt and pepper. Saute 3 to 4 minutes. Cover pan and cook over low heat about 15 minutes.

Preparation time: 30 minutes
Baking time: 20 minutes
Servings: 4 to 5

Pasta and
Zucchini Casserole

Slices of crisp sauteed zucchini between layers of creamy pasta make a delicious casserole.

6 ozs. tubetti **or** salad macaroni
4 medium zucchini
2 eggs
2 tbs. water
flour
1/4 to 1/3 cup olive oil
3 tbs. butter
6 small green onions, sliced
3 tbs. flour

2 cups milk
1/2 tsp. dry mustard
salt to taste
1/4 tsp. white pepper
1 cup grated Swiss cheese
1/2 cup thinly sliced salami,
   dried beef **or** crumbled bacon
1/4 cup grated Parmesan cheese

Cook pasta according to package directions. Rinse and drain well. Cut zucchini lengthwise into 1/4-inch slices. Beat eggs and water together. Dip zucchini slices first in flour then in beaten egg. Heat olive oil in a large skillet. Saute zucchini a few slices at a time. Drain on paper towels. Melt butter in small saucepan. Saute green onions 2 to 3 minutes until soft. Add 3 tablespoons flour. Cook, stir-

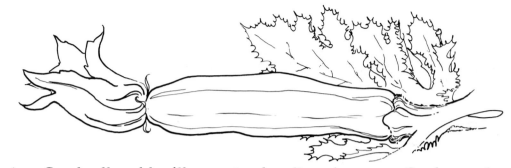

ring 2 minutes. Gradually add milk, mustard, salt and pepper. Cook over low heat, stirring constantly, until sauce thickens. Add cheese. Reserve one-fourth of this cheese sauce. Mix remaining sauce with cooked pasta. In a 9- by 9-inch buttered baking dish, place one layer of sauteed zucchini. Cover with one-half of the pasta and one-half cheese sauce. Sprinkle with one-half of the salami strips. Top with a layer of zucchini, the rest of the pasta mixture, salami and remaining zucchini slices. Pour reserved cheese sauce over top and sprinkle with Parmesan cheese. Bake uncovered in 350°F. oven 15 to 20 minutes until hot and bubbly. Allow to stand 10 minutes after remonving from oven. Cut in squares to serve.

Variation: Use 1/3 cup diced canned green chiles in addition to or in place of salami strips.

Pasta With Seafood

Curried Pasta With Mussels 120
Pasta With Crab 114
Pasta With Easy Tuna Sauce 128
Pasta With Mexican Fish Sauce 122
Pasta With Red Clam Sauce 116
Pasta With Salmon 118
Pasta With Scallops And Red Peppers 110
Pasta With Scallops And Walnuts 112
Pasta With Shrimp And Dill Sauce 113
Pasta With White Clam Sauce 115
Seafood And Pasta Stew 126
Shrimp Chow Mein 124

Pasta With Seafood

Seafood and pasta are another natural alliance. There may be as many different kinds of seafood available as there are pasta shapes.

Always choose the freshest seafood available because anything less will detract from the dish. It is important not to cook fish or shellfish too long. Seafood needs cooking only to firm its flesh. To avoid overcooking, most of the following recipes call for adding the fish or shellfish when the sauce is almost done, or sauteing it separately and then combining it with the pasta just before serving.

The pretty green of spinach pasta (page 32) is particularly attractive with pale scallops or sole, or the pink of shrimp or salmon. We like to pair the more delicate sauces with thinner pasta shapes or the small shells or corkscrews. Lemon pasta (page 35) and seafood make a wonderful combination.

Most of the delicious dishes in this section are quick to prepare. Four which take somewhat longer, but are worth the effort, are Curried Pasta with Mussels, Shrimp Chow Mein, the hearty Seafood and Pasta Stew and a Spanish-style fish sauce.

Pasta with
Scallops and Red Peppers

Preparation time: 30 minutes
Servings: 3 to 4

Red peppers are a pleasant contrast to the pasta and scallops in flavor as well as visually.

12 ozs. fresh pasta **or** 8 ozs. dried pasta
2 medium size fresh red bell peppers
2 tbs. butter
3 tbs. minced shallots
1 cup cream

1/4 tsp. white pepper
1 lb. scallops, cut in half if large size
salt to taste
2 tbs. butter for pasta
2 tbs. minced parsley

This is a very fast sauce, so time the pasta to be done approximately 6 minutes after you start the sauce. Cut red peppers along ridges and remove membrane and seeds. Using a swivel blade vegetable peeler, remove outer skin from pepper sections. Cut in thin slivers or julienne. Melt butter in medium skillet. Saute shallots 1 minute. Add cream and white pepper. Turn heat on high and reduce cream 2 to 3 minutes until it starts to thicken. Reduce heat to medium. Add scallops and salt. Cook 1 minute. Add red peppers and cook 1 minute. Toss hot, well-drained pasta with 2 tablespoons butter and about half of the scallop mixture. Top with remaining scallops and parsley. Serve on warm plates.

Pasta with
Scallops And Walnuts

For a pretty contrast with the scallops use thin green pasta or Red Pepper Pasta, page 33.

12 ozs. fresh pasta **or** 8 ozs.
   dried pasta
1 / 4 cup chopped walnuts **or**
   toasted bread crumbs
1 lb. scallops
4 tbs. butter

2 cloves, garlic, minced
red pepper flakes to taste
grated rind from 1 / 2 lemon
1 tbs. lemon juice
2 tbs. melted butter
2 tbs. minced parsley

Cook pasta while preparing sauce. Drain well. Toast walnuts in a 300°F. oven for 5 or 6 minutes until they are slightly browned. Set aside. Cut scallops in half horizontally. Melt butter in a large skillet. Saute scallops, garlic and red pepper flakes for approximately 2 minutes. Add lemon rind and juice. Toss cooked, well-drained pasta with 2 tablespoons melted butter. Add scallops, walnuts and parsley and toss until mixed. Serve immediately on warm plates.

Wine suggestion: Chardonnay or Pinot Blanc

Pasta with
Shrimp And Dill Sauce

Preparation time: 15 minutes
Servings: 3 to 4

This delicate sauce is lightly flavored with dill. Use fettuccine or wider egg noodles for the pasta.

12 ozs. fresh pasta **or** 8 ozs. dried pasta
3/4 cup yogurt
1/4 cup heavy cream
1 tbs. soy sauce
1 tsp. Worcestershire sauce
1/2 tsp. dry mustard
1/2 tsp. dried dill weed **or** 1 tbs. fresh dill, finely chopped
1/4 tsp. white pepper
1/2 lb. small, cooked, shelled shrimp

Cook pasta while you are making the sauce. drain well. Gently heat yogurt, cream, soy sauce, Worcestershire, dry mustard, dill and pepper. Do not allow to boil. Add shrimp and heat to serving temperature. Toss with hot well-drained pasta and serve immediately on warm plates.

Wine suggestion: Chardonnay or Sauvignon Blanc

Pasta with
Crab

Use green fettuccine or Red Pepper Pasta, page 33, for this quick and pretty seafood pasta.

12 ozs. fresh pasta **or** 8 ozs. dried pasta
3 tbs. butter
2 tbs. minced shallots
6 to 8 fresh mushrooms, sliced
1/2 tsp. grated fresh ginger
1/2 cup half and half

3 ozs. cream cheese, cut in small cubes
1-1/2 cups flaked crab meat
dash cayenne pepper
salt and pepper to taste
2 tbs. minced parsley
2 tbs. melted butter

Have pasta cooking water hot and time the pasta to be done when sauce is ready. Drain well. Melt butter in a medium size skillet. When foaming add shallots, mushrooms and fresh ginger. Saute 3 to 4 minutes until mushrooms are done. Add half and half and cream cheese. Increase heat and cook 2 to 3 minutes until sauce starts to thicken. Add crab meat, cayenne, salt and pepper. Cook only until crab is hot, stirring as little as possible. Toss hot, well-drained pasta with butter. Top with sauce and serve immediately on warm plates.

Wine suggestion: Pinot Blanc or Dry Semillon

Pasta with
White Clam Sauce

Clams cooked with white wine and garlic make a delicious quick pasta sauce.

1 lb. fresh pasta **or** 12 ozs.
   dried pasta (linguine)
1/4 cup butter
1 to 2 large cloves garlic, minced
2 tbs. flour
2 cans (6-1/2 ozs. ea.) chopped clams

1/4 cup dry white wine **or** dry vermouth
half and half
1/4 parsley, finely chopped
1/2 tsp. dried thyme
salt and pepper to taste

Heat pasta cooking water in large pot. Melt butter in small saucepan. Add garlic and cook one minute. Stir in flour and cook two minutes. Drain clams, reserving juice. Combine reserved clam juice and white wine. Add enough half and half to make 2 cups liquid. Add to flour mixture gradually and cook until sauce thickens slightly. Add parsley, thyme, salt and pepper. Simmer for approximately 10 minutes. Cook pasta while sauce is simmering. Add clams to sauce and heat to serving temperature. Combine with hot, well-drained pasta and serve immediately on warm plates.   *Wine suggestion: Sauvignon Blanc or Chardonnay*

Pasta with
Red Clam Sauce

Any firm-fleshed fish such as halibut or rock cod can be substituted for the clams.

12 ozs. fresh pasta **or** 8 ozs. dried pasta
1 tbs. olive oil
1 small onion, finely chopped
1 clove garlic, minced
1 can (28 ozs.) Italian-style tomatoes
1/2 tsp. anchovy paste (optional)
2 tbs. tomato paste
2 tsp. sugar
1/2 tsp. **each** dried sweet basil, thyme and oregano
2 cans (6-1/2 ozs. ea.) chopped or minced clams
salt and pepper to taste

Time pasta to be done when sauce is ready. Heat oil in medium size saucepan. Add onion and garlic and saute 4 to 5 minutes until onion is translucent. While onions are cooking, empty tomatoes into sieve over a bowl. Cut tomatoes in half.

Squeeze out most of the seeds. Trim away hard core and chop tomatoes coarsely. Add tomatoes and 1/2 cup of the tomato juice to saucepan. (Reserve remaining tomato juice for another use.) Add anchovy paste, tomato paste, sugar, sweet basil, thyme and oregano to saucepan. Drain clams. Set clams aside and add clam juice to saucepan. Bring to boil. Cook uncovered over medium heat for approximately 20 minutes until sauce reduces and starts to thicken. Add clams and heat. Serve immediately over hot, well-drained pasta on warm plates.

Note: If fish is substituted for clams, lightly flour the fish and saute in 2 to 3 tablespoons olive oil. Cut into cubes and add to tomato sauce.

Wine suggestion: Dry Riesling or Sauvignon Blanc

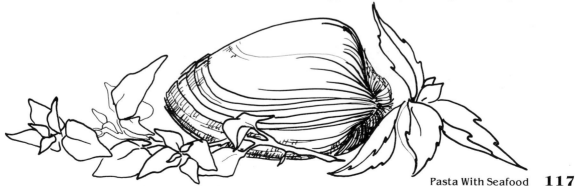

Pasta with
Salmon

This is a delicately flavored dish. It also makes an excellent first course. Use fresh poached salmon if available.

12 ozs. fresh pasta **or** 8 ozs.
   dried pasta
4 tbs. butter
3 tbs. minced shallots
1 cup heavy cream **or** yogurt
1-1/2 to 2 cups fresh cooked **or**
   canned salmon
1 tsp. prepared horseradish

2 to 3 tbs. chopped fresh dill
1 tbs. minced parsley
1/4 tsp. white pepper
1 tbs. fresh lemon juice
salt to taste
2/3 cup freshly grated
   Parmesan cheese

Cook pasta while preparing sauce. Drain well. Melt butter in large skillet. Add shallots and saute 1 to 2 minutes until soft. Stir in cream. Bring to boil and cook 2 to 3 minutes until cream starts to thicken. Flake salmon into 1/2- to 1-inch pieces. Add along with remaining ingredients. Heat through. Pour over hot, drained pasta. Serve immediately on warm plates.

Wine suggestion: Sauvignon Blanc or Dry Riesling

Red Clam Sauce (page 116) ▶

Curried Pasta With Mussels

The light curry flavor is delightful with both the pasta and the mussels. Clams are also delicious in this dish.

12 ozs. fresh **or** 8 ozs. dried linguine
3 to 4 dozen mussels
5 tbs. olive oil
1/4 tsp. dried hot red pepper flakes
1/2 cup dry white wine **or** vermouth
1/4 cup heavy cream
1 large onion, thinly sliced
1 large clove garlic, minced
1-1/2 tsp. curry powder
1 cup fresh tomato pieces
salt and pepper to taste
1/3 cup chopped roasted peanuts

Have the pasta cooking water hot and time the pasta to be done when the sauce is ready. Drain well. Scrub the mussels with a stiff brush and remove beards. Wash well. Heat 2 tablespoons olive oil in a large skillet or heavy pot. Add the pepper flakes and saute for a minute. Add mussels and wine. Cover the pot and cook over high heat 3 to 4 minutes, or until the shells have all opened. Shake the pan occasionally while the mussels are steaming. Remove from heat and let cool. When cool enough to handle, remove the mussels from the shells. Reserve one or two shells for garnishing individual plates or a few for a large serving bowl. Strain 3/4 cup mussel liquid through cheesecloth into a measuring cup. Add 1/4 cup heavy cream. Heat 3 tablespoons olive oil in a large skillet. Add onion slices and cook until onion is soft and translucent, but not browned. Add garlic and curry powder to onion. Cook 2 minutes. Add tomato pieces, cream-mussel juice mixture, salt and pepper. Cook over high heat 3 to 4 minutes until cream starts to thicken. Add mussels to sauce and just heat through. Mix one half of the sauce with hot, well-drained pasta. Top with remaining sauce and chopped peanuts. Garnish with reserved mussel shells. Serve immediately.

Wine suggestion: Chenin Blanc or Riesling.

Pasta with
Mexican Fish Sauce

The hearty flavors of tomato and red pepper complement sea bass, rock cod or other firm-fleshed fish.

12 ozs. fresh pasta **or** 8 ozs. dried pasta (shells or bowties)
1 can (28 ozs.) Italian-style tomatoes
1 large red pepper, peeled, seeded, and chopped
2 tbs. olive oil
1 small onion, finely chopped
1 large clove garlic, minced
1 tbs. anchovy paste
1 lb. sea bass **or** rock cod
1 tbs. lemon juice
salt and pepper to taste
2 tbs. butter
Parmesan cheese

Have pasta cooking water hot and time pasta to be done when sauce is ready. Drain well. Drain tomatoes in a sieve. Reserve juice and discard seeds. Cut out hard core of tomato and coarsely chop. Peel, seed and chop pepper. Heat olive oil in heavy saucepan. Add onion and cook 3 to 4 minutes until soft but not brown. Add pepper, garlic and anchovy paste. Cook over low heat for 2 minutes. Add reserved tomato juice. Reduce over high heat until approximately one half of original volume. Cut fish into 1-inch squares. Add fish, lemon juice and tomatoes to saucepan. Simmer gently 2 to 3 minutes until fish is just done. Do not over-cook. Toss cooked, well-drained pasta with 2 tablespoons butter and add sauce. Serve immediately on warm plates. Pass freshly grated cheese.

Wine suggestion: Well chilled white jug wine

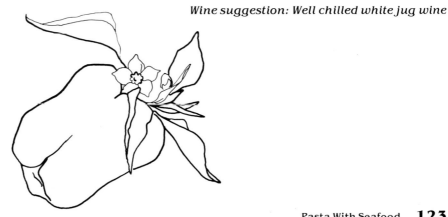

Shrimp Chow Mein

This classic Chinese dish goes together very quickly after the shrimp are prepared and the vegetables sliced.

6 ozs. fresh Chinese noodles **or** 4 ozs. dried noodles **or** spaghettini
2 tsp. cornstarch
1 tbs. **plus** 1 tsp. soy sauce
1 egg white
1/4 tsp. white pepper
6 ozs. small raw shrimp, peeled, deveined, and cut in half lengthwise
6 tbs. vegetable oil
1 large clove garlic, peeled and flattened
1/4-inch slice fresh ginger
3 green onions, white part only, thinly sliced
6 ozs. small mushrooms, thinly sliced
6 ozs. fresh bean sprouts **or** thinly sliced raw cabbage
1 tsp. sesame oil

Cook noodles and drain well. Combine cornstarch, 1 teaspoon soy sauce, egg white and white pepper. Pour over shrimp. Mix well and set aside. Add 2 table-spoons oil to wok or large non-stick frying pan. Add garlic and ginger. Cook over high heat until slightly brown. Remove garlic and ginger and discard. Add cooked noodles to frying pan. Stir to coat with oil and allow to lightly brown on all sides. Turn out onto a plate covered with paper towels. Add 2 more tablespoons oil to frying pan. When hot add shrimp mixture. Stir quickly for a minute or two until shrimp are opaque and firm. Turn out onto another plate covered with paper towels. Add remaining 2 tablespoons vegetable oil to frying pan. When hot, add onion and mushrooms and stir for a minute or two. Add bean sprouts and toss quickly. Return shrimp and cooked noodles to frying pan and toss. Remove from heat and sprinkle with remaining 1 tablespoon soy sauce and the sesame oil. Stir quickly and serve immediately on warm plates.

Variation: Uncooked chicken cut into 1/2-inch cubes can be substituted for the shrimp.
Wine suggestion: Chenin Blanc or Riesling

Seafood And Pasta Stew

4 ozs. dried pasta (small shells **or** fettuccine broken in short pieces)
2 lbs. assorted seafood: scallops, shrimp, clams, mussels, sea bass,
    halibut **or** rock cod
5 tbs. olive oil
1 large onion, finely chopped
2 medium carrots, coarsely grated
1 large celery stalk, finely chopped
3 garlic cloves, minced
1/4 tsp. hot red pepper flakes, or to taste
3 to 4 medium size tomatoes, peeled, seeded and chopped
1 tsp. dried oregano
1/2 tsp. dried thyme
1 cup dry white wine **or** dry vermouth
1/4 cup minced parsley
1 cup frozen peas
salt and pepper

Cook pasta. Rinse, drain and set aside to be reheated at the last minute in the stew. Wash scallops. Peel and devein shrimp. Scrub the clams and mussels. Cut fish in 1-1/2-inch pieces. Heat oil in a large, non-aluminum frying pan. Add onion, carrot, celery, garlic and hot pepper flakes. Saute over medium heat 4 to 5 minutes until vegetables are soft and lightly browned. Add tomato pieces, oregano, thyme, and wine. Simmer uncovered for 5 minutes. Add white fish pieces, clams, or mussels. Cover and simmer 3 minutes. Turn white fish pieces over in the sauce and add scallops, shrimp and peas. Cook for 2 minutes. Add parsley and cooked pasta. Simmer for 1 minute to reheat pasta. Serve in large heated bowls.

Wine suggestion: French Colombard or Dry Riesling

Pasta with
Easy Tuna Sauce

This satisfying sauce can be easily prepared with ingredients usually found in your cupboard.

12 ozs. fresh pasta **or** 8 ozs. dried
   small shells, corkscrews or tagliarini
2 tbs. butter
4 green onions, thinly sliced
2 tbs. flour
1-1/4 cups milk
1 tsp. Worcestershire sauce

1/2 cup grated sharp cheddar cheese
2 cans (6-1/2 ozs. ea.) water-packed
   tuna, well drained
3 tbs. minced parsley
1/2 cup canned crisp onion rings **or**
   1 cup cherry tomatoes, cut in half
   and seeded

Cook pasta while you are making the sauce. Time the pasta to be done just when the sauce is ready. Melt butter in medium saucepan. Saute green onions for 1 to 2 minutes. Stir in flour. Cook for 2 minutes. Gradually add milk and cook, stirring constantly, until sauce starts to thicken. Add Worcestershire sauce, cheddar cheese and drained tuna. Cook until heated through. Toss with hot, well- drained pasta. Serve immediately on warm plates. Garnish with parsley, onion rings or cherry tomatoes.

Seafood and Pasta Stew (page 126) ▶

Pasta With Chicken And Meat

Broccoli And Canadian Bacon In Shells 140
Chicken With Italian Sausages And Pasta 134
Chicken With Savory Noodle Stuffing 133
Indian Style Chicken And Macaroni 136
Jumbo Shells With Chicken 138
Pasta With Bolognese Sauce. 146
Pasta With Meat Sauce. 148
Pasta With Meatball Sauce 150
Pasta With Quick Ham And Cheese Sauce 145
Pasta With Sausage Sauce 152
Spicy Pork And Noodles 142
Walnut Chicken And Noodle Casserole. 132

Pasta With Chicken And Meat

Pasta makes a welcomed substitute for rice or potatoes when added to meat or chicken dishes and there is no limit to wonderful combinations. Some of our zesty favorites are Chicken and Italian Sausages with Pasta and Indian Chicken and Macaroni with its blending of delicious spices. For a truly outstanding treat, make Old Fashioned Chicken and Noodles with your own freshly made noodles (see Finest Egg Noodles, page 27).

Meats of all kinds go extremely well with pasta. We have included a quick ham and cheese dish, several hearty meat sauces, such as our Bolognese Sauce which was inspired by the one served at Harry's American Bar in Venice, Italy, and Spicy Pork and Noodles, a piquant and satisfying stir-fry dish.

Substitute different kinds of pastas for rice or potatoes in your favorite casseroles and wait for the compliments.

Preparation time: 30 minutes
Baking time: 20 to 25 minutes
Servings: 4 to 6

Walnut Chicken And Noodle Casserole

Crunchy walnuts add an interesting texture to this creamy chicken and noodle casserole. Make this with leftover turkey or roast chicken.

12 ozs. fresh **or** 8 ozs. dried wide noodles
   or linguine
7 tbs. butter
5 tbs. flour
3 cups chicken broth
1/3 cup dry sherry **or** white wine
1/2 tsp. paprika

1/2 tsp. salt
1/4 tsp. pepper
8 ozs. fresh mushrooms, sliced
2 to 2-1/2 cups diced cooked chicken
1/2 cup coarsely chopped walnuts
Parmesan cheese

Cook pasta. Drain well and place in a large buttered casserole. Melt 5 table-spoons butter in saucepan. Add flour. Cook, stirring, 2 minutes. Gradually add chicken broth, sherry, paprika, salt and pepper. Cook, stirring constantly, until sauce thickens. Melt remaining butter in a medium skillet. Saute mushrooms 4 to 5 minutes. Combine mushrooms, chicken and walnuts with pasta in casserole. Add sauce. Mix carefully. Top with Parmesan cheese. Bake at 350°F. for 20 to 25 minutes until hot and bubbly. *Wine suggestion: Chardonnay, Sauvignon Blanc or Dry Riesling*

Preparation time: 20 minutes
Roasting time: 1 hour 15 min.
Servings: 4 to 6

Chicken with
Savory Noodle Stuffing

Buttery egg noodles, spinach and sausage make a savory stuffing for roast chicken. Roasting chicken at this high temperature produces a crisp brown skin.

3 ozs. medium dried egg noodles
3 tbs. butter
3/4 cup finely diced celery
4 to 6 green onions, thinly sliced
1 clove garlic, minced

6 ozs. fresh spinach, coarsely chopped
3/4 cup diced cooked Italian or link sausage
salt
1/4 tsp. white pepper
1 roasting chicken, 4 to 4-1/2 lbs.

Cook noodles according to package directions. Drain well. Melt butter in skillet. Saute celery, onions and garlic until soft but not brown. Stir in spinach and saute until wilted. Add diced sausage, drained noodles, salt and pepper. Mix well. Stuff chicken and tie with kitchen string. Roast on a rack in a 450°F. oven for approx. 1 hour and 15 minutes. Pour a small amount of water in bottom of roasting pan to keep juices from burning. Let rest 10 minutes before carving.

Wine suggestion: Chardonnay, Sauvignon Blanc, light Zinfandel or Merlot

Chicken with
Italian Sausages And Pasta

Tender nuggets of chicken and mild Italian sausages make a delicious hearty pasta main course.

8 ozs. dried pasta (small bow ties or fettuccine)
3 mild or hot Italian sausages
1/4 cup white wine **or** water
3 chicken breast halves, skinned and boned
flour, salt and pepper to coat chicken
2 tbs. butter
3 tbs. minced shallots
1 cup chicken broth
1/2 cup tomatoes, peeled, seeded and chopped
2 to 3 tbs. coarsely chopped pimiento
salt and pepper to taste
2 tbs. minced parsley

Place sausages and white wine in a small saucepan. Cover and bring to a boil. Simmer 5 minutes. Uncover and prick sausages to release fat. Increase heat to

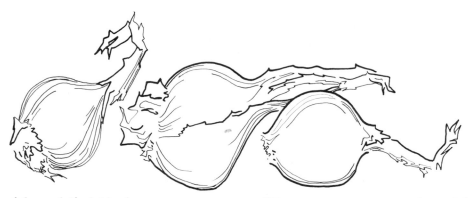

evaporate liquid and lightly brown sausages. When sausages cool, cut into 1/2-inch rounds. Cut chicken breasts into 1-inch squares. Dust lightly with seasoned flour. Melt butter in medium size skillet over medium heat. When foaming, add chicken and saute until lightly browned, about 2 minutes on each side. Remove from pan. Reduce heat to low and add shallots. Stir for a minute. Add chicken broth and stir to remove browned bits from bottom of pan. Bring to boil. Add chicken pieces, sausages, chopped tomato, pimiento, salt and pepper. Stir for 1 minute to heat through. Place hot, drained pasta in a large heated bowl. Add sauce and toss to combine. Sprinkle with parsley. Serve immediately on warm plates.

Wine suggestion: Chardonnay or Cabernet Blanc

Preparation time: 30 minutes
Baking time: 20 minutes
Servings: 4

Indian-Style Chicken and Macaroni

1-1/2 cups macaroni **or** tubetti
4 chicken breast halves
3 to 4 tbs. butter
1/4 cup minced green onions
1 clove garlic, minced
2 tbs. flour
1-3/4 cups chicken broth
1 cup sour cream

1/4 tsp. **each** cinnamon, coriander,
 ginger, pepper and cumin seed
1/2 tsp. ground cardamom
1/2 tsp. salt
1 tsp. soy sauce
1/4 tsp. Tabasco, or to taste
grated lemon rind
3 tbs. toasted sesame seeds

Cook pasta as directed on package. Skin and bone chicken. Melt butter in medium skillet. Saute chicken breasts over medium heat 3 to 4 minutes each side. Remove from skillet and set aside. Add green onions and garlic to pan. Cook a minute or two. Stir in flour and cook another minute. Add chicken broth. Cook, stirring, until sauce thickens. Add sour cream, cinnamon, coriander, cumin, cardamom, ginger, pepper, salt, soy sauce, Tabasco and lemon rind. Mix well. Place well-drained pasta in buttered casserole. Top with chicken breasts. Pour sour cream sauce over chicken. Sprinkle with sesame seeds. Bake 350°F. oven 15 to 20 minutes until hot and bubbly. *Wine suggestion: Dry Riesling or Sauvignon Blanc*

Jumbo Shells with Chicken (page 138) ▶

Preparation time: 30 minutes
Cooking time: 20 to 25 minutes
Servings: 4

Jumbo Shells Stuffed With Chicken

8 ozs. jumbo shells
Chicken Nut Filling

Gruyere and Sherry Sauce, page 139
Parmesan cheese

Cook shells as directed. Drain and rinse with cold water. Prepare filling and sauce as directed. Stuff shells with filling mixture using a small spoon. Place stuffed shells in buttered individual ramekins or a large casserole. Top with sauce. Sprinkle with Parmesan cheese. Bake in 350°F. oven until heated through and bubbly. Place under broiler to lightly brown. Serve immediately.

CHICKEN NUT FILLING

1-1/2 cups cubed cooked chicken
1/2 cup coarsely chopped pecans
4 tbs. finely chopped parsley
1 egg

1 cup ricotta cheese
3 tbs. Parmesan cheese
1/2 tsp. salt
white pepper

Mix ingredients together well. Stuff cooked shells with mixture.

GRUYERE AND SHERRY SAUCE

2 tbs. butter
1/4 cup minced shallots
3 tbs. flour
1-1/4 cups chicken broth
1/4 cup dry sherry
1/2 tsp. salt
white pepper
1/2 cup grated Gruyere cheese **or** Swiss cheese
1/4 cup heavy cream

Melt butter in small saucepan. Stir in shallots and cook one minute. Add flour and cook 2 minutes. Gradually add chicken broth and sherry. Cook over low heat stirring constantly until sauce thickens. Remove from heat. Stir in salt, pepper, grated cheese and cream. Spoon over filled shells.

Shells With
Broccoli And Canadian Bacon

Stuffed shells arranged in an oven-to-table serving dish make an attractive buffet or potluck main course.

8 manicotti shells
Cheese Sauce, page 141
1 tbs. butter
4 green onions, thinly sliced
1 cup diced Canadian bacon **or** cooked ham
1 cup ricotta cheese
4 tbs. Parmesan cheese
1 egg
1/2 tsp. salt
2 cups coarsely chopped cooked broccoli

Cook pasta shells in boiling water according to package directions. Drain and rinse in cold water for easier handling. Drain again. Prepare cheese sauce as directed. Melt butter in small skillet. Saute onions for a minute or two to soften. Add Canadian bacon pieces and cook for another minute or two. In a small bowl combine ricotta, Parmesan, egg and salt. Mix well. Add bacon mixture, chopped broccoli and 1/2 cup cheese sauce. Use a teaspoon to stuff shells with filling. Place stuffed shells in buttered ovenproof baking dish or individual au gratin dishes. Spoon remaining cheese sauce over shells. Bake in 350ºF. oven 15 minutes until hot and bubbly. Place under broiler to lightly brown.

CHEESE SAUCE

3 tbs. butter
3 tbs. flour
2 cups milk
1-1/2 tsp. Worcestershire sauce
3/4 cup grated Swiss cheese
salt and pepper

Melt butter in small saucepan. Add flour and cook, stirring for 2 minutes. Gradually add milk and Worcestershire sauce. Cook, stirring constantly until sauce thickens. Add cheese, salt and pepper. Stir to blend. Use as directed.

Spicy Pork With Noodles

This is a zesty stir-fry dish. Chicken or shrimp can be substituted for pork.

1 lb. Chinese noodles
1-1/2 lbs. pork cutlets
1-1/2 tbs. cornstarch
2 tbs. **each** soy sauce and dry sherry
7 tbs. vegetable oil
1 lb. fresh mushrooms, sliced
1 clove garlic, minced
6 green onions, thinly sliced
1 green pepper, coarsely chopped
1/2 tsp. dried red pepper flakes (or to taste)
2 cups chicken broth
1 tsp. sesame oil
1 package (10 ozs.) frozen peas, cooked

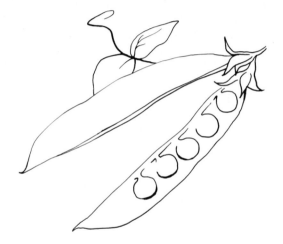

Cook noodles according to package directions. Drain and set aside. Slice pork into 1/4- by 1-inch matchsticks. Combine sliced pork with cornstarch, soy sauce and sherry. Let stand 10 to 15 minutes. Heat 4 tablespoons oil in large frying pan or wok. Saute mushrooms 4 to 5 minutes. Remove from frying pan and set aside. Heat 3 tablespoons oil in same frying pan or wok. When very hot, add marinated pork, green onions, green pepper, garlic and red pepper flakes. Stir constantly 3 to 4 minutes until pork is cooked. Remove mixture from frying pan and pour off any remaining oil. Stir in chicken broth. Bring to boil. Scrape brown bits from bottom of pan. Add mushrooms, pork mixture, sesame oil and cooked noodles. Cook, stirring, a few minutes until all ingredients are hot. Stir in peas. Serve in a large warm bowl.

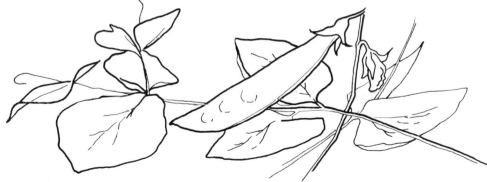

Pasta with
Quick Ham And Cheese Sauce

Use corkscrews or linguine with this easy sauce.

12 ozs. fresh pasta **or** 8 ozs. dried pasta
2 tbs. butter
3 green onions, thinly sliced
2 tbs. flour
1-1/4 cups milk
1/2 tsp. dry mustard
few drops Tabasco

3/4 cup grated sharp cheddar cheese
3/4 cup diced cooked ham
1/4 cup sliced stuffed green olives
   or chopped pimiento, well drained
3 tbs. minced parsley
Parmesan cheese

Cook the pasta while you are making the sauce. Time the pasta to be done just when the sauce is ready. Melt butter in a medium saucepan. Add onions and saute 1 to 2 minutes. Stir in flour and cook for 2 minutes. Gradually add milk. Cook, stirring constantly, over low heat until sauce starts to thicken. Add dry mustard, Tabasco and cheese. Toss with hot, well-drained pasta. Add ham, olives and parsley. Toss again. Serve immediately on warm plates. Pass freshly grated Parmesan cheese.

◄ **Broccoli and Canadian Bacon in Shells** (page 140)

Preparation time: 15 minutes
Cooking time: 30 minutes
Servings: 6

Pasta with
Bolognese Sauce

The Bolognese sauce served at Harry's American Bar in Venice, Italy, was the inspiration for this recipe.

1 lb. fresh pasta **or** 12 ozs. dried pasta
2 tbs. oil
1 medium onion, finely chopped
1 medium carrot, finely chopped
1 small stick celery, finely chopped
1 lb. lean ground beef
1 cup tomato sauce
1 cup beef broth
1/2 cup dry red wine
1/2 tsp. dried oregano
1/2 tsp. dried sweet basil
salt and pepper to taste

Have pasta cooking water hot so it can be quickly brought to a full boil when needed. Time the pasta so it will be done when sauce is ready. Heat oil in a large

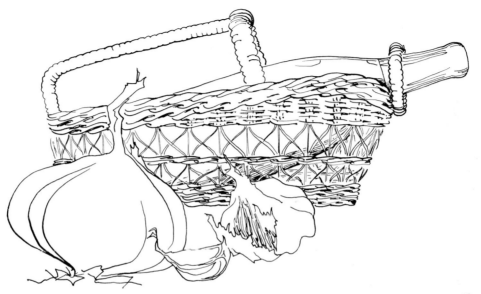

heavy saucepan. Add onion, carrot, celery and meat. Saute over medium-high heat until meat is lightly browned. Break meat into fine pieces as it browns. Add tomato sauce, broth, wine, oregano, sweet basil, salt and pepper. Bring to boil. Reduce heat and simmer uncovered for about 30 minutes until the sauce has thickened. Serve over hot, well-drained pasta. Sprinkle with cheese.

Wine suggestion: Barbera or Cabernet Sauvignon

Preparation time: 15 minutes
Cooking time: 30 minutes
Servings: 4 to 5

Pasta with
Meat Sauce

This is a fresh-tasting sauce to make when tomatoes are out of season.

1 lb. fresh **or** 12 ozs. dried pasta
1 can (28 ozs.) Italian-style tomatoes
2 tbs. tomato paste
1 can (8 ozs.) tomato sauce
2 tsp. sugar
1 tbs. dried sweet basil
1/2 tsp. dried marjoram
1/2 cup dry white wine **or** vermouth

1/2 tsp. salt
1/4 tsp. pepper
1/2 lb. ground beef
1 small onion, finely chopped
1 clove garlic, minced
1/4 cup chopped green pepper
1 tbs. olive oil
6 to 8 fresh mushrooms, sliced

Have pasta cooking water hot so it can be quickly brought to a full boil when needed. Time the pasta so it will be done just when the sauce is ready. Drain tomatoes in a sieve over a bowl. Cut tomatoes in half and squeeze out most of the seeds. Trim out any hard stem. Discard seeds. Chop tomatoes coarsely. Put strained tomato juice and chopped tomatoes in a large saucepan. Bring to boil. Add tomato paste, tomato sauce, sugar, sweet basil, marjoram, wine, salt and pepper. Bring to boil. Simmer over very low heat, stirring occasionally. Brown ground beef in a skillet. Break into small pieces as it cooks. Using a slotted spoon, remove ground beef from skillet and add to tomato mixture. Pour off all but one table-spoon of fat in skillet. Add onions, garlic and green pepper and saute until soft. Add to tomato sauce. Heat olive oil in skillet. Saute mushrooms 4 to 5 minutes. Add to sauce. Simmer slowly uncovered 25 to 30 minutes. Serve over hot, well-drained pasta on warm plates.

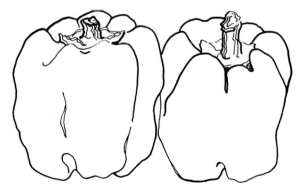

Preparation time: 20 minutes
Cooking time: 30 minutes
Servings: 4 to 5

Pasta with
Meatball Sauce

Here is a hearty meatball and tomato sauce for pasta. Use the food processor to crumble the crackers. It does the job fast and with no crumbs on the floor!

1 lb. fresh pasta **or** 12 ozs. dried pasta

Meatballs:
1 lb. ground beef
2 eggs
2 tbs. finely chopped parsley
1/4 cup finely chopped onion
2 tbs. grated Parmesan cheese
1/2 tsp. salt, or to taste
1/2 tsp. pepper
10 soda crackers, finely crumbled
1/3 cup olive oil

Sauce:
1/4 cup chopped onion
1 clove garlic, minced
1 can (14 ozs.) Italian-style tomatoes
1 can (8 ozs.) tomato sauce
1 can (10-1/4 ozs.) beef gravy
1 tsp. Italian herb seasoning
salt and pepper to taste

Have pasta cooking water hot so it can be quickly brought to a full boil when needed. Time the pasta so it will be done just when the sauce is ready. In a large

mixing bowl combine ground beef, eggs, parsley, onion, Parmesan, salt, pepper and soda crackers. Mix well. Shape into 1-1/2- to 2-inch meatballs. Heat olive oil in large skillet. Brown meatballs on all sides. Remove from skillet and set aside. Make sauce. Pour all but one tablespoon oil from pan. Saute chopped onion and garlic in oil until soft. Drain tomatoes in a sieve. Squeeze out seeds and remove hard cores. Discard seeds. Coarsely chop tomatoes. Add tomatoes and their juice, tomato sauce, beef gravy, herb seasoning, salt and pepper to skillet. Bring to boil. Add meatballs to sauce. Reduce heat to very low and simmer meatballs in sauce uncovered for about 30 minutes. Serve over hot, well-drained pasta on warm plates.

Preparation time: 15 minutes
Cooking time: 30 minutes
Servings: 3 to 4

Pasta with
Sausage Sauce

This is an excellent sauce to make ahead. It goes together very quickly if you use a food processor to chop the onion, green pepper and sausage meat.

12 ozs. fresh pasta **or** 8 ozs. dried pasta
4 mild **or** hot Italian sausages
1 small yellow onion, finely chopped
1 small green pepper, finely chopped
1 can (28 ozs.) Italian-style tomatoes

1/3 cup dry red wine
2 tsp. dried oregano
salt and pepper to taste
2 tbs. parsley, minced

Have pasta cooking water hot and time pasta so it will be done when sauce is ready. Remove sausage casings. Flatten sausages to about 3/8-inch thick. Place in cold skillet and quickly brown on both sides. Remove from pan and pour out all but 2 tablespoons of fat. Add onion and green pepper to skillet. Cook over low heat 3 to 4 minutes until softened. While onion and peppers are cooking, drain tomatoes in sieve over a bowl. Cut out the tough stem ends and squeeze out most of the seeds. Coarsely chop tomatoes and sausages. Add tomatoes and their juice, chopped sausages, wine, oregano, and salt and pepper to skillet. Simmer uncovered 30 minutes. Serve over hot, well-drained pasta on warm plates.

Spicy Pork and Noodles (page 142) ▶

Traditional Favorites

Armenian Pilaf 178
Baked Noodle Pudding 179
Cannelloni. 160
Chicken And Noodles 172
Chicken And Sausage Filling For Ravioli 168
Coconut And Peanut Crescents 180
Four Cheese Macaroni 171
Homemade Ravioli. 164
Lasagne. 158
Manicotti. 156
Pasta Omelet 176
Pasta Souffle. 174

Traditional Favorites

Included in this section are those wonderful old favorites such as ravioli, cannelloni, manicotti and lasagne, which may take a little longer to prepare, but are too special to omit.

Homemade ravioli are fun to make and professional results can be achieved with our directions and an inexpensive ravioli mold or individual ravioli stamp.

All of these delicious recipes make ideal dishes for a buffet or pot luck supper. They can be prepared ahead and frozen, allowing you to plan the extra preparation time needed at your convenience.

Preparation time: 45 minutes
Baking time: 20 minutes
Servings: 4

Manicotti

Cheese and spinach filled manicotti shells are topped with a zesty tomato sauce. Serve with a crisp salad and hot French bread.

8 manicotti shells
3 tbs. butter
1 cup finely chopped onion
1 small clove garlic, minced
1 can (15 ozs.) tomato sauce
1 tsp. dried sweet basil
1/2 tsp. dried oregano
salt and pepper
1/2 cup cooked chopped spinach

1-1/2 cups ricotta cheese
1 cup grated Swiss cheese
1/4 cup finely chopped parsley
1/2 tsp. salt
1/4 tsp. white pepper
4 to 6 drops Tabasco
dash nutmeg
Parmesan cheese for topping

Cook manicotti shells as directed on package. (If using Stuff-a-roni shells, cook them for 6 minutes in large pot of boiling water.) Drain and rinse in cold water for easier handling.

Melt butter in saucepan. Saute onion and garlic until soft but not brown. Place one-half of mixture in mixing bowl. Set aside. To remaining onion in saucepan

add tomato sauce, basil, oregano, salt and pepper. Simmer over low heat 20 to 25 minutes to blend flavors. Combine cooked, well-drained spinach with reserved onion-garlic mixture. Add ricotta, Swiss cheese, parsley, salt, pepper, Tabasco and nutmeg. Mix well.

Stuff shells with cheese spinach mixture using a teaspoon or iced-tea spoon. Place in large buttered baking dish or individual au gratin dishes, allowing two shells per serving. Top with tomato sauce and sprinkle with Parmesan cheese. Bake in 375°F. oven for 20 minutes or until hot and bubbly.

This dish can be assembled ahead, covered and refrigerated. Allow an extra 15 minutes' baking time.

Preparation time: 45 minutes
Baking time: 30 minutes
Servings: 6 to 8

Lasagne

Meat Sauce, page 159   homemade lasagne noodles, page 21,
Cheese Sauce   **or** 1 pkg. lasagne noodles

Prepare sauces as directed. Cook noodles and drain. Rinse with a little cold water for easier handling. Place one layer of cooked noodles in buttered 9- by 13-inch baking dish. Cover noodles with a layer of meat sauce. Cover meat sauce with layer of cheese sauce. Repeat layers. Finish with cheese sauce. Bake lasagne uncovered in a 325°F. oven until hot and bubbly, about 30 minutes. Let stand 10 minutes before serving.

CHEESE SAUCE

4 tbs. butter   3 tbs. flour   3/4 cup grated Parmesan cheese
1 small onion, chopped   2 cups milk   2 egg yolks

Melt butter in saucepan. Saute onion 2 to 3 minutes. Add flour and cook 2 minutes. Gradually add milk. Cook, stirring, until sauce thickens. Add Parmesan, salt and pepper. Blend a little of the hot sauce into the egg yolks. Gradually add the warmed egg yolks to sauce. Cook over very low heat 10 minutes, stirring constantly.

MEAT SAUCE

1-1/2 lbs. ground beef
1 large onion, chopped
1 clove garlic, minced
1/4 cup parsley, minced
1 can (28 ozs.) Italian-style tomatoes

1 can (6 ozs.) tomato paste
1 bay leaf
1/4 tsp. **each** salt and pepper
1 tsp. dried oregano
1/3 cup red wine

Brown beef in large skillet. Break into small pieces as it cooks. Drain off fat. Add onion, garlic and parsley. Cook until onion starts to soften. Drain tomatoes into a sieve. Squeeze out seeds and cut out hard core. Coarsely chop tomatoes. Add tomatoes and juice, tomato paste, bay leaf, salt, pepper, oregano, and wine to meat mixture. Bring to boil. Simmer uncovered over low heat 45 minutes. If sauce seems thin, turn up heat for a few minutes.

Preparation time: 1 hour
Baking time: 35 minutes
Servings: 6

Cannelloni

Fresh homemade pasta squares (see basic recipe on page 16) make the best cannelloni, but packaged manicotti tubes can be used if desired.

Chicken and Mushroom Filling, page 162
Tomato Sauce, page 163
Cheese Sauce, page 163
18 fresh pasta squares, page 21

If desired, filling and sauces can be made ahead and refrigerated. When ready to use, warm sauces over low heat. Make pasta squares and cook immediately after cutting to prevent their drying out. Cook in rapidly boiling water about 8 minutes. Remove from water and cover with wet paper towels. To assemble cannelloni place 2 to 3 tablespoons of filling on the bottom third of each square. Roll into a cylinder. Place rolls seam side down in one large or two smaller well- buttered baking dishes. Spoon tomato sauce over rolls and top with cheese sauce. Bake at 350°F. 20 minutes until hot and bubbly. Cannelloni can be frozen before baking. Allow to defrost in refrigerator. Bake 35 to 40 minutes at 350°F. Cover with foil the first 20 minutes.

Pasta with Scallops and Walnuts (page 112) ▶

CHICKEN AND MUSHROOM FILLING

4 to 5 tbs. olive oil
2 to 2-1/2 lbs. chicken thighs
1 large onion, finely chopped
2 carrots, finely chopped
1 clove garlic, minced
1 cup white wine

1/2 lb. fresh mushrooms
1/2 cup finely chopped parsley
1 egg
1 tsp. salt
1/2 tsp. pepper
1/2 cup Parmesan cheese

Remove skin from chicken. Heat 2 to 3 tablespoons oil in large skillet. Brown chicken on both sides. Remove from pan. Add onion, carrot and garlic to remaining oil in skillet. Saute until onion is soft. Scrape up brown bits from bottom of skillet. Return chicken pieces to skillet. Add wine. Bring to boil. Reduce heat and simmer covered 45 minutes. Remove from heat. When cool enough to handle remove chicken from bones. Heat remaining oil in another skillet. Saute mushrooms 4 to 5 minutes. Add mushrooms to chicken and finely chop in a food processor. Combine mixture with parsley, egg, salt, pepper and Parmesan.

TOMATO SAUCE

1 tbs. olive oil
1/2 cup chopped onion
1 can (14 ozs.) beef broth

1 can (14 ozs.) tomato puree
1/4 cup Madeira or Marsala
1/2 tsp. oregano

1 tsp. sweet basil
1/2 tsp. sugar

Saute onion in olive oil until soft. Add remaining ingredients. Bring to boil. Cook uncovered over medium heat 20 to 25 minutes until sauce reduces and thickens.

CHEESE SAUCE

3 tbs. **each** butter and flour
2 cups milk

1/2 cup Parmesan cheese
1 tsp. salt

1/4 tsp. white pepper
dash nutmeg

Melt butter in small saucepan. Stir in flour and cook 3 minutes. Gradually add milk. Cook until sauce thickens. Stir in remaining ingredients. Cook 3 to 4 minutes.

Preparation time: 45 minutes
Cooking time: 10 minutes
Makes: 4 dozen

Homemade Ravioli

Ravioli are little squares or circles of flat pasta filled with meat, cheese or spinach, and served with a sauce or melted butter and cheese. They can be made with a ravioli form which turns out 10 or 12 at a time, **or** they can be stamped out individually with a single ravioli cutter or a round cookie cutter, **or** the can be made freeform on a large sheet of pasta using a kitchen knife to cut the squares. There is also a slotted or ridged rolling pin which marks the filled ravioli squares for cutting.

Start by preparing your filling, then refrigerate it so that it has a chance to stiffen for easier handling. This step is particularly important if you are using a cheese filling made with ricotta cheese. **Then make your pasta dough—using the basic homemade pasta recipe on page 16. Roll out the dough as thinly as possible. Do not let it dry,** because it becomes difficult to fill and cut. Cover the portion of dough not being used with a damp towel to prevent it from drying out.

If you are using a ravioli form, cut the dough into strips approximately one-inch wider and one-inch longer than the form. If it is a two-part form, flour the metal frame and place one strip of dough over the top. Place the other half of the form which has small indentations in it, directly on top of the pasta dough. Press down lightly to mark filling depressions, and remove form. Place a small amount of filling, usually 1/2 to 1 teaspoon depending on size of the ravioli, in each depression. Overfilling may cause them to break open during cooking. Brush edges of each ravioli with a little water. A pastry brush works well for this. Place another strip of dough over top of filling. Gently press down dough along ridges of the ravioli form. With a heavy rolling pin, roll across ravioli form two or three times to cut dough into individual squares. They will not come completely apart with this rolling. Gently turn ravioli out of the form, flat side down onto a floured cookie sheet. Cover with a towel and let rest an hour before cooking. As the ravioli dry they will break apart easily.

If you are using a single ravioli or cookie cutter, cut as many squares or circles as possible out of the dough. Place a small amount of filling on half of the squares or circles. Brush edges with a little water. Place another square or circle directly on top of filling and firmly press each ravioli around the edges. Place on a floured cookie sheet or plate, cover with a towel, and let rest an hour before cooking. Ravioli will expand in size during cooking, so if you have a large cutter you

Continued

may wish to make triangles or half circles from one piece of cut dough rather than using two pieces to form the ravioli.

To make ravioli without a form, cut a straight line across the top of dough with a knife or fluted pastry cutter. Place small amounts of filling approximately 1-1/2 inches apart, 2-1/2 inches down from the cut edge. Brush dough with a little water in a straight line below filling and in between the fillings, making square outlines. Fold down cut edge over filling. Press down firmly along bottom edge of folded over pasta dough and then cut out individual ravioli as uniformly as possible. Using a fork, press edges together well to be sure a good seal is formed. Using the bottom line you have just cut for the top of the dough, continue placing filling 1-1/2 inches apart, 2-1/2 inches down from the top edge, and repeat the moistening and cutting process until you have used all the filling. Place ravioli on a floured cookie sheet or plate, cover, and let rest an hour before cooking. After raviolis are made, they may be frozen or refrigerated prior to cooking.

To cook ravioli bring 6 to 8 quarts of water to a rapid boil. Add 1 tablespoon salt. Drop in ravioli and cook for 10 to 12 minutes, depending on thickness of dough and size. Drain well and pour into a heated bowl. Cover with sauce or

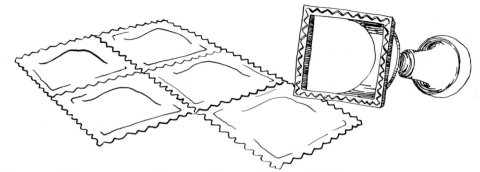

melted butter and Parmesan cheese. Serve immediately.

If desired, cooked ravioli can be added to beef or chicken broth and served as a hearty soup.

Ravioli fillings can be made with a wide variety of foods. Chicken, leftover roast beef, veal, clams, spinach and cheese used alone or in combinations make good fillings. Cooked meat should be minced or ground and then seasoned and mixed with beaten egg to hold the filling together. Classic ravioli fillings tend to be very lightly seasoned so they are complemented with flavorful tomato sauces or pesto. Try making fillings and sauces with your favorite foods.

Here are two of our favorite ravioli fillings, one using chicken, and the other a savory cheese mixture. Try cheese ravioli with Creamy Nut Sauce, page 52, or Pesto, page 48.

Chicken and Sausage Filling For Ravioli

1-1/2 cups diced cooked chicken
1 mild or hot Italian sausage, cooked
1 egg
3 tbs. chopped parsley
1/2 tsp. salt
1/4 tsp. pepper
1/2 tsp. Worcestershire sauce
1/4 cup Parmesan cheese

Put chicken and sausage through meat grinder twice, or chop very, very fine by hand or using food processor. Combine with egg, parsley, salt, pepper, Worcestershire and cheese. Refrigerate until you are ready to fill ravioli. Makes filling for approximately 4 dozen ravioli.

Cheese Filling For Ravioli

1-1/2 cups ricotta cheese
1 cup grated Parmesan cheese
1/4 cup minced parsley
2 eggs
1/2 tsp. salt
1/4 tsp. white pepper
dash nutmeg
1/2 tsp. grated lemon rind

Combine all ingredients in a small bowl. Mix until smooth. Refrigerate until ready to fill ravioli. Makes filling for approximately 4 dozen ravioli.

Four-Cheese Macaroni

Preparation time: 30 minutes
Servings: 4

1 pkg. (16 ozs.) macaroni
1 cup milk
1 cup cottage cheese
3 eggs
1/2 tsp. salt

1/8 tsp. white pepper
1/2 tsp. dry mustard
1-1/3 cups grated sharp cheddar cheese
1-1/3 cups grated Swiss cheese
1/2 cup grated Parmesan cheese

Cook macaroni according to package directions. Drain well. In a blender or food processor container place milk, cottage cheese, eggs, salt, pepper, mustard, and nutmeg. Blend for a few seconds until well combined. Place one-third of cooked macaroni in a buttered casserole. Top with one-third each of the cheddar and Swiss cheeses. Add another layer of macaroni and another third of the cheese. Add remaining macaroni. Pour egg and milk mixture over macaroni. Add remaining grated cheese. Sprinkle Parmesan over top. Bake in a 375°F. oven 20 minutes, or until hot and bubbly.

◀ **Chicken with Italian Sausages and Pasta** (page 134)

Preparation time: 3 hours
Finishing time: 30 minutes.
Servings: 4 to 6

Chicken And Noodles

For a real old-fashioned treat to be shared with good friends, make your own fresh noodles using the recipe for Finest Egg Noodles on page 27. It is definitely worth the extra effort. If possible, prepare the chicken and stock one day, and make the pasta and finish the dish the next or make the pasta a few days ahead and keep refrigerated.

1 lb. fresh noodles **or** 12 ozs. dried pasta
1 stewing chicken, about 5 lbs.
1 large carrot, sliced
1 large onion, sliced
1 stalk celery, sliced
1/2 cup dry white wine
2 qts. water
1/2 tsp. thyme

1 bay leaf
6 to 8 peppercorns
2 to 3 parsley sprigs
salt and pepper
2 tbs. butter
1/2 lb. fresh mushrooms, sliced
2 to 3 tbs. chopped pimientos

If you make the noodles ahead, keep well wrapped and refrigerated until needed. Cut chicken into pieces and place in large heavy pot with carrot, onion, celery, wine and water. Tie thyme, bay leaf, peppercorns and parsley in small piece of cheesecloth. Add to pot. Bring to boil, cover, and simmer over low heat 3 hours until chicken is tender. Remove chicken pieces from stock. When cool enough to handle remove chicken from bones and discard skin and bones. Cut chicken into 3/4- to 1-inch cubes. Refrigerate until you are ready to assemble dish. Strain stock through a coarse sieve. If possible, chill stock for several hours or overnight for easy removal of fat, or place in freezer until fat solidifies. Bring degreased chicken stock to boil. Cook uncovered over high heat until stock is reduced to one quart. Saute sliced mushrooms in butter 4 to 5 minutes. Set aside. Bring large pot of water to boil. Cook fresh noodles one minute to remove surface starch. Drain immediately and rinse. Bring chicken stock back to boil. Add noodles, cubed chicken and mushrooms. Cook uncovered about 5 minutes if using fresh noodles, or 8 to 10 minutes if using dried pasta. Season with salt and pepper. Garnish with pimiento. Serve in soup plates.

Pasta Souffle

Use leftover cooked pasta, or cook and drain two ounces dried pasta to make a great brunch or luncheon entree.

2 ozs. cooked pasta, cut in one-inch pieces
3 tbs. butter
3 tbs. flour
1 cup milk
1 tsp. Worcestershire sauce
1 tsp. dry mustard
1/2 cup sharp cheese, grated (cheddar **or** Gruyere)
1/3 cup diced ham (optional)
1/4 cup Parmesan cheese
4 eggs, separated
1/8 tsp. white pepper
salt to taste

Melt butter in medium size saucepan. Add flour and cook 2 minutes. Add milk and cook over low heat, stirring constantly, until sauce starts to thicken. Add

Worcestershire sauce, mustard, cheese, diced ham, 2 tablespoons Parmesan cheese, white pepper and salt. Remove pan from heat. Beat egg whites until stiff. Beat egg yolks in small bowl. Carefully stir a little of the hot cheese mixture into the egg yolks to warm them. Stir warmed yolks into the sauce. Fold in stiffly beaten egg whites. Pour into 4 buttered individual souffle dishes or use a buttered ovenproof platter. Sprinkle with remaining 2 tablespoons Parmesan cheese. Bake in a 375°F. oven for 15 minutes, or until lightly browned and puffy. Serve immediately.

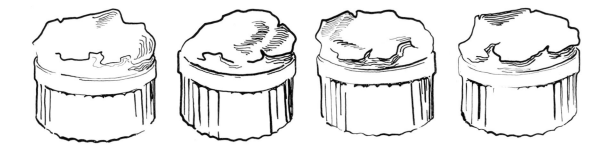

Pasta Omelet

This is another good way to use leftover cooked pasta.

1-1/2 cups cooked pasta,
   cut in small lengths
2 tbs. olive oil
5 eggs
2 green onions, thinly sliced
2 tbs. parsley

1/4 cup tomato pieces
1/3 cup prosciutto, finely
   chopped **or** coarsely chopped
   peanuts
2 tbs. Parmesan cheese

Heat olive oil in a 10-inch skillet. Add cooked pasta, spreading it in a thin cake. Saute 6 or 7 minutes until pasta is lightly browned on one side. Beat eggs. Add onions, parsley, tomato and prosciutto to egg mixture. Pour over pasta. Cook on top of stove until eggs start to set. Sprinkle with Parmesan cheese. Place under pre-heated broiler in oven and cook until lightly browned and puffy. Slip out of pan onto a paper towel lined plate. Place another plate upside down over the omelet. Invert omelet onto second plate. Cut into wedges to serve.

Pepperoni and Mushroom Sauce (page 53) ▶

Preparation time: 15 minutes
Baking time: 30 minutes
Servings: 4 to 6

Armenian Pilaf

This classic pilaf goes perfectly with lamb shish kebob.

3 cans (14 ozs. ea.) chicken broth
8 tbs. butter (one cube)
1/2 cup crushed fine egg noodles
2 cups uncooked long grain rice

Bring chicken broth to boil in saucepan. Melt 4 tablespoons butter in a 3-quart flameproof casserole with tightly fitting lid. Add crushed noodles to melted butter and stir until golden brown. Add boiling broth and rice. Stir gently. Boil 5 minutes. Cover casserole and place in a 350°F. oven 20 to 25 minutes, or until all liquid is absorbed. Stir gently and dot with remaining butter. Return to oven and bake uncovered for 5 minutes. Serve immediately.

Preparation time: 15 minutes
Cooking time: 40 minutes
Servings: 6

Baked Noodle Pudding

Thin egg noodles are baked with applesauce, nuts, apricot jam and a sour cream topping for a Hungarian-style dessert.

6 ozs. thin egg noodles
2 tbs. melted butter
3/4 cup applesauce
1/2 cup white raisins
1/2 cup finely chopped walnuts
1/4 cup brown sugar
1/4 tsp. cinnamon

1/3 cup apricot jam
3 eggs
1/4 cup sugar
1/2 cup sour cream
1/2 tsp. vanilla
dash nutmeg
pinch salt

Cook noodles according to directions. Drain well and place in mixing bowl. Immediately add melted butter, applesauce, raisins, walnuts, brown sugar and cinnamon. Mix gently and pour into a buttered 1-1/2-quart souffle or baking dish. Spread jam over mixture. Beat remaining ingredients together until well combined. Pour over noodles. Bake uncovered in a 350°F. oven 40 minutes, until custard has puffed and pudding is firm and bubbling. Serve hot.

Coconut And Peanut Crescents

These are traditional Chinese New Year dessert won ton.

1/3 cup sweetened flaked coconut
1/3 cup chopped Spanish peanuts
2 tbs. sugar
30 to 35 **round** won ton wrappers
deep fat for frying

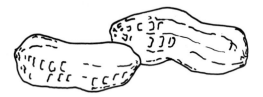

Combine coconut, peanuts and sugar. Make crescents one at a time. (Keep unused won ton wrappers covered with a damp towel.) Moisten top half edge of wrapper with a little water. Place 1 level teaspoon of coconut mixture in center of wrapper. Fold and bring edges together. Press firmly. Heat fat to 375°F. Fry crescents a few at a time until they are puffy and golden brown. Sprinkle with additional sugar and serve hot.

Variation: Almonds, cashews or pecans can be substituted for peanuts.

Glossary

Agnolotti — Round ravioli usually stuffed with a meat filling.

Bucatini — Hollow pasta tubes, a little thicker than spaghetti.

Cannelloni — Large hollow tubes or squares of sheet pasta, stuffed, rolled into cylinders and baked.

Cappelletti — Called "little hats" because of their round cap shape.

Conchiglie — Also called "sea shells." Fluted shell shaped pasta either ridged or smooth. Available in many sizes. The larger sizes can be stuffed.

Farfalle — Butterfly or bowshaped pasta available in many sizes.

Fettuccine — Ribbon noodles about 1/4-inch wide, served with a wide variety of sauces, the most familiar being Fettuccini Alfredo.

Fusilli — Spiral-shaped spaghetti strands.

Gnocchi — A small fluted shell, or dumpling made of flour, semolina or potatoes.

Lasagne — A wide flat noodle baked in layers with meat or vegetable filling.

Linguine — Very narrow flat noodles.

Macaroni — This is the Italian word for all dried pasta. The common usage means pasta tubes, which can be short, long, thick, thin, curved or straight.

Manicotti — Either a large 4-inch long, 1-inch diameter tube, or a square of flat pasta which is stuffed, rolled into a cylinder and baked.

Noodles — Ribbons of flat pasta available in widths from 1/8-inch to over 1-inch.

Orecchiette — Small ear-shaped pieces of pasta.

Pansotti — A stuffed dumpling similar to ravioli, usually triangular in shape.

Ravioli — A well-known square pasta dumpling stuffed with various meat, cheese or vegetable fillings.

Rigatoni — Hollow macaroni tubes about 1/2-inch in diameter by 2 inches.

Spaghetti — Thin, solid round pasta strings, any length.

Spaghettini — A thinner variety of spaghetti.

Rote — Wheel-shaped pasta.

Tagliatelle — Flat egg noodles approximately 1/2-inch to 5/8-inch wide.

Tagliarini — A thinner version of Tagliatelle.

Tortellini — Small ring or half-moon-shaped stuffed pasta.

Trenette — Genoa name for a narrower and thicker tagliatelle noodle.

Tubetti — Short tubular pasta, also known as salad macaroni.

Tubettini — Shorter version of tubetti, approximately 1/4-inch long.

Vermicelli and Vermicellini — Thin spaghetti, sometimes sold in curled or cluster form.

Ziti — Smaller and smoother type of rigatoni, about 1/2-inch thick.

Equivalents

Dairy

2 tbs. **butter, margarine** or **oil** = 1 oz.

2 ozs. **butter, margarine** or **oil** = 1/4 cup

2 tbs. **butter** = 2 tbs. melted butter

1 stick **butter** = 4 ozs. = 8 tbs. = 1/2 cup

3/4 cup **butter** = 12 tbs. = 1-1/2 sticks

1 lb. **butter** = 2 cups = 32 tbs. = 4 sticks

1 oz. **cheese** = 1/4 cup lightly packed shredded cheese

2 ozs. **cheese** = 1/2 cup lightly packed shredded cheese

4 ozs. **cheese** = 1 cup lightly packed shredded cheese

5 large **whole eggs** = 1 cup

8 large **egg whites** = 1 cup

12 large **egg yolks** = 1 cup

1 **egg white** = 2 tbs.

1/3 cup **instant nonfat dry milk** + 3/4 cup water = 1 cup nonfat milk

1 tbs. **whipping cream** + 3 tbs. milk = 1/4 cup half and half

1 cup **whipping cream**, whipped = 2 cups

1 cup **buttermilk** = 1 cup yogurt for baking
1 cup **buttermilk** for baking = 1 tbs. lemon juice **or** vinegar **plus** milk **to equal**
   1 cup

Vegetables

5 to 6 medium **carrots** = 1 lb. = 1-1/2 cups shredded
1/4 lb. fresh **mushrooms** = about 1-1/4 cups sliced
1 small **onion** weighs about 1/4 lb. = 1/2 to 2/3 cup chopped
1 tbs. **instant minced onion** = 1/4 cup minced fresh onion
1 whole **green onion** = 1 tbs. minced or sliced
1 medium **tomato** weighs 1/4 to 1/3 lb. = 1/2 cup chopped
1/4 cup **tomato paste** + 3/4 cup water = 1 cup tomatoes for cooking
1/4 cup **tomato paste** + 1/4 cup water = 1/2 cup tomato sauce
1/2 cup **tomato sauce** + 1/2 cup water = 1 cup tomato juice for cooking
1 tbs. finely-minced **fresh herbs** = 1 tsp. dried herbs
1 tbs. lightly-packed, minced **fresh parsley** = 1 tsp. dried parsley

Fruit

1 medium **lemon** yields 3 tbs. juice + 2 tsp. grated peel
1 medium **orange** yields 1/4 to 1/2 cup juice + 4 tsp. grated peel
3 to 4 **bananas** = 1 lb. = 1-3/4 cups mashed
1 lb. **apples** = 3 cups sliced
1 lb. seedless **raisins** = 2-3/4 cups

Miscellaneous

1 average **bread slice** = 1/2 cup soft breadcrumbs
1 average **bread slice** = 1/4 cup fine dry breadcrumbs
1 oz. sliced or chopped **nuts** = 1/4 cup
1 lb. **granulated sugar** = 2 cups
1 cup **granulated sugar** = 8 ozs.
1 lb. **brown sugar** = 2-1/4 cups
1 cup **brown sugar** = 6 ozs.

1 lb. **powdered sugar** = 4 cups

1 cup **powdered sugar** = 4-1/2 ozs.

1 cup **honey** = 1-1/4 cups granulated sugar + 1/4 cup water

1 oz. **chocolate** = 1 sq. = 4 tbs. grated

1 oz. **unsweetened chocolate** = 3 tbs. cocoa + 1 tbs. butter or oil

1 oz. **unsweetened chocolate** + 4 tsp. sugar = 1-2/3 oz. semisweet chocolate

3 tbs. **cocoa** + 1 tbs. butter or oil = 1 oz. unsweetened chocolate

1 cup uncooked **macaroni** = 2-1/4 cups cooked

1 cup uncooked **noodles** = about 1-1/4 cups cooked

1 lb. **spaghetti** (12-inch pieces) = 6-1/2 cups cooked

1 cup uncooked long grain or brown **rice** = 3 cups cooked

1 lb. **lentils** = 2-1/4 cups = 5 cups cooked

1 lb. **split peas** = 2-1/4 cups = 5 cups cooked

1 lb. **kidney beans** = 2-1/2 cups = 6 cups cooked

1 lb. **pinto beans** = 2-1/2 cups = 6 cups cooked

1 lb. **navy beans** = 2 cups = 5 cups cooked

Index

Appetizers
    Clam and Spinach. 59
    Green Chile and Cheese 60
    Won Ton 58
Armenian Pilaf 178
Artichoke and Tortellini Salad 73
Basic Homemade Egg Pasta 16
Bell Peppers and Anchovy Sauce 45
Blue Cheese and Pasta Salad 74
Bobbie's Walnut Sauce 51
Broccoli and Canadian Bacon In Shells. . . . 140
Butter and Cheese Sauce. 39
Calamari and Dill Pasta Salad. 84
Cannelloni. 160
Carrot Pasta 30
Cheese
    Filling for Ravioli 169
    Sauce for Cannelloni 163
    Sauce for Lasagne 158
Clam and Spinach Appetizers. 59
Chicken Dishes
    Cannelloni. 160

Chicken and Noodles 172
Chicken and Savory Noodle Stuffing 133
Chicken with Italian Sausage and Pasta . 134
Indian Style Chicken and Macaroni 136
Jumbo Shells with Chicken. 138
Walnut Chicken and Noodle Casserole . . 132
Chicken
    and Mushroom Filling for Cannelloni . . . 162
    and Sausage Filling for Ravioli 168
Classic Garlic and Oil Sauce 38
Coconut and Peanut Crescents 180
Confetti Pasta. 92
Crab With Pasta 114
Creamy Nut Sauce 52
Curried Pasta With Mussels 120
Deli Pasta Salad 82
Egg
    Noodles, Finest 27
    Pasta, Homemade. 16
    Pasta With Semolina Flour. 28
Fettuccine Alfredo 42
Four-Cheese Macaroni. 171

Four-Cheese Sauce. 44
Fresh Tomato and Garlic Sauce 47
Garlic and Oil Sauce. 38
Gorgonzola Sauce, Creamy. 43
Green Chile and Cheese Appetizer. 60
Green Chile Pasta. 34
Hot Dogs and Wagonwheels 80
Homemade Pastas
    Carrot. 30
    Egg With Semolina Flour 28
    Finest Egg Noodles. 27
    Green Chile 34
    Lemon 35
    Red Pepper. 33
    Spinach 32
    Whole Wheat 29
Homemade Ravioli. 164
Indian Style Chicken and Macaroni 136
Jumbo Shells With Chicken 138
Lasagne. 158
Lemon Pasta 35
Lemon Pasta Soup 65

Macaroni Salad 76
Manicotti. 156
Meat Sauce for Lasagne 159
Mexican Pasta Soup 68
Mushroom Pasta Soup 66
Noodle Pudding, Baked. 179
Oriental Noodle Salad 78
Oriental Noodle Soup. 61
Parsley Sauce 50
Pasta
    and Cheese Soup. 69
    In Broth 64
    Omelet 176
    Oriental 101
    Primavera 96
    Provencal 94
    Salad with Green Beans and Walnuts. 77
    Shells with Green Beans and Sardines. . . . 83
Pasta With
    Souffle 174
    Bolognese Sauce 146
    Carrots and Broccoli 88

Easy Tuna Sauce. 128
Fresh Zucchini. 91
Marinara Sauce 98
Meat Sauce 148
Meatball Sauce 150
Mexican Fish Sauce 122
Peas and Mushrooms 90
Quick Ham and Cheese Sauce 145
Red Clam Sauce 116
Rich Mushroom Sauce 100
Salmon. 118
Sausage Sauce 152
Scallops and Red Peppers 110
Scallops and Walnuts. 112
Shrimp and Dill Sauce 113
White Clam Sauce. 115
Patio Shell Salad. 75
Pepperoni and Mushroom Sauce, Spicy 53
Pesto Sauce. 48
Pork and Noodles, Spicy 142
Ravioli, Homemade 164
Red Pepper Pasta 33

Salads
Artichoke and Tortellini. 73
Blue Cheese Pasta. 74
Calamari and Dill 84
Deli Pasta. 82
Green Beans and Sardines. 83
Green Beans With Walnuts. 77
Hot Dogs and Wagonwheels 80
Macaroni 76
Oriental Noodle. 78
Patio Shell 75
Seafood and Pasta Stew 126
Seafood Dishes
Calamari and Dill Salad 84
Curried Pasta with Mussels 120
Easy Tuna Sauce. 128
Mexican Fish Sauce 123
Pasta with Crab. 114
Pasta with Salmon 118
Pasta with Scallops and Red Peppers . . . 110
Pasta with Scallops and Walnuts 112
Red Clam Sauce 116

Sardines and Green Bean Salad 83
Seafood and Pasta Stew. 126
Shrimp and Dill Sauce 113
Shrimp Chow Mein 124
White Clam Sauce. 115
Soup
    Lemon Pasta 65
    Mexican Pasta 68
    Mushroom Pasta. 66
    Oriental Noodle. 61
    Pasta and Cheese Soup 69
    Pasta In Broth 64
    Won Ton 62
Spaghetti Carbonara 54
Spicy Pepperoni and Mushroom Sauce 53
Spicy Pork and Noodles. 142
Spinach and Mushroom Pasta 102
Spinach Pasta 32
Tomato
    and Hot Pepper Sauce, Zesty. 46
    Sauce for Cannelloni 163
    Sauce for Vegetable Lasagne 105

Vegetable Lasagne 104
Vegetable Sauce for Lasagne 105
Walnut Chicken and Noodle Casserole 132
White Wine and Butter Sauce 40
Whole Wheat Pasta 29
Won Ton Soup 62
Zucchini and Pasta Casserole 106

METRIC CONVERSION CHART

Liquid or Dry Measuring Cup (based on an 8 ounce cup)

1/4 cup = 60 ml
1/3 cup = 80 ml
1/2 cup = 125 ml
3/4 cup = 190 ml
1 cup = 250 ml
2 cups = 500 ml

Liquid or Dry Measuring Cup (based on a 10 ounce cup)

1/4 cup = 80 ml
1/3 cup = 100 ml
1/2 cup = 150 ml
3/4 cup = 230 ml
1 cup = 300 ml
2 cups = 600 ml

Liquid or Dry Teaspoon and Tablespoon

1/4 tsp. = 1.5 ml
1/2 tsp. = 3 ml
1 tsp. = 5 ml
3 tsp. = 1 tbs. = 15 ml

Temperatures

°F		°C
200	=	100
250	=	120
275	=	140
300	=	150
325	=	160
350	=	180
375	=	190
400	=	200
425	=	220
450	=	230
475	=	240
500	=	260
550	=	280

Pan Sizes (1 inch = 25 mm)

8-inch pan (round or square) = 200 mm x 200 mm
9-Inch pan (round or square) = 225 mm x 225 mm
9 x 5 x 3-inch loaf pan = 225 mm x 125 mm x 75 mm
1/4 inch thickness = 5 mm
1/8 inch thickness = 2.5 mm

Pressure Cooker

100 Kpa = 15 pounds per square inch
70 Kpa = 10 pounds per square inch
35 Kpa = 5 pounds per square inch

Mass

1 ounce = 30 g
4 ounces = 1/4 pound = 125 g
8 ounces = 1/2 pound = 250 g
16 ounces = 1 pound = 500 g
2 pounds = 1 kg

Key (America uses an 8 ounce cup - Britain uses a 10 ounce cup)

ml = milliliter
l = liter
g = gram
K = Kilo (one thousand)
mm = millimeter
m = milli (a thousandth)
°F = degrees Fahrenheit

°C = degrees Celsius
tsp. = teaspoon
tbs. = tablespoon
Kpa = (pounds pressure per square inch)
This configuration is used for pressure cookers only.

Metric equivalents are rounded to conform to existing metric measuring utensils.

Confetti Pasta (page 92)